Hotel Sale Promotion

STRATEGIES TO IMPACT REVENUE AND INCREASE OCCUPANCY

Joe Wolosz

INFINITE CORRIDOR PUBLISHING
SAN FRANCISCO, CALIFORNIA

Hotel and Motel Sales, Marketing and Promotion

STRATEGIES TO IMPACT REVENUE
AND INCREASE OCCUPANCY

By Joe Wolosz

Published by:

Infinite Corridor Publishing
Post Office Box 640051
San Francisco, CA 94164-0051 USA

All rights reserved. No part of this book may be reproduced or transmitted in any form or by any means, electronic or mechanical, including photocopying, recording or by any information storage and retrieval system without written permission from the author, except for the inclusion of brief quotations in a review.

Copyright © 1997
by Joe Wolosz
First Printing 1997
Printed in the United States of America

Library of Congress Catalog Card Number: 97-70853
Wolosz, Joe
     Hotel and motel sales, marketing and promotion: strategies to impact revenue and increase occupancy/ by Joe Wolosz. – 1st ed.

ISBN 0-9657298-9-3

Dedication

To my father and mother, Joe and Maxine.
They can be held responsible for my enchantment with
the hospitality industry.

Table of Contents

CHAPTER 1 WELCOME 11
   COMPELLING REASONS TO CREATE A PLAN 11
   TRENDS AFFECTING THE LODGING INDUSTRY 13
   THE MARKETING PLAN 16
   ADOPT THE SPIRIT OF THE ENTREPRENEUR 17
   NOW IS THE TIME TO TAKE ACTION 18
   WHAT YOU NEED TO KNOW TO BEGIN 20
   SOME DEFINITIONS DEFINED 22
   RESEARCH METHODOLOGY 23
   HOW THE MATERIAL IS ORGANIZED IN THIS BOOK 25
   ON YOUR MARK... 26

CHAPTER 2 RESEARCH: MAKING THE INFORMATION MEANINGFUL 27
   BEGINNING YOUR STUDY 27
   ANALYSIS OF YOUR PROPERTY; OCCUPANCY, RATE AND REVPAR. 28
   LOOKING TO THE FUTURE THROUGH THE USE OF YIELD MANAGEMENT 32
   THE YIELD STATISTIC 36
   EXPLORING YOUR PROPERTY THROUGH QUANTITATIVE AND QUALITATIVE ANALYSIS. 37
   ANALYSIS OF THE COMPETITION 40
   THE MARKETING MIX 43
   ANALYSIS OF THE MARKET 44

CHAPTER 3 IDENTIFYING AND SELECTING YOUR TARGET MARKETS 51
   SOURCES OF BUSINESS 51
   LOCATING USERS FOR YOUR PROPERTY 56
   LESSONS FROM YOUR COMPETITION 56
   REPOSITIONING 57
   PRICING 60

CHAPTER 4 PROMOTION 63
   AN ONGOING EFFORT 63
   A LOOK AT YOUR PRINTED MATERIAL 64
   ADVERTISING AND PROMOTING ON-PROPERTY 71

SPECIALTY ADVERTISING ... 72
PACKAGES ... 73
DIRECT MAIL ... 76
E-MAIL, THE WORLD WIDE WEB AND THE INTERNET ... 84
GETTING IN THE GUIDE BOOKS ... 90
PROMOTIONAL STRATEGY ... 92

CHAPTER 5 SALES AND SELLING ... 93

MARKETING COMPARED TO SELLING ... 93
EMOTIONS DICTATE PURCHASE DECISIONS ... 95
WORD OF MOUTH ... 97
PROFILE OF THE PROFESSIONAL SALESPERSON ... 98
CULTIVATING LEADS ... 103
SPEAKING WITH CLIENTS ... 112
IN PERSON SALES CALLS ... 116
NEGOTIATING RATES ... 117
ORGANIZING YOUR ACCOUNTS ... 120

CHAPTER 6 OFFERING EXCEPTIONAL SERVICE FOR REPEAT BUSINESS ... 123

EXCEED YOUR GUESTS EXPECTATIONS ... 123
AMENITIES ... 125
BASICS ... 126
COMMENT CARDS AND COMPLAINTS ... 130
THOSE WHO BOOK YOUR PROPERTY ... 132

CHAPTER 7 ASSIGNING THE RIGHT OBJECTIVES, STRATEGIES AND TACTICS TO YOUR PLAN ... 135

YOUR RESEARCH DEVELOPS INTO YOUR PLAN ... 135
THE REASONS SOME PLANS DO NOT SUCCEED ... 136
THE MISSION STATEMENT ... 138
PREPARING OBJECTIVES ... 139

CHAPTER 8 ACTION PLAN: BREAKING EVERYTHING DOWN INTO SMALL STEPS ... 145

YOUR ACTION PLAN DEFINED ... 145
COMFORT IN SECURITY ... 146

CHAPTER 9 BUDGETING ... 151

WHEN TO SET YOUR BUDGET ... 151
ADOPT THE TASK APPROACH ... 152

CHAPTER 10 SALES AND MARKETING PLAN ... 157

YOU HAVE MADE IT 157
WHAT YOU HAVE ACCOMPLISHED 158
SALES AND MARKETING PLAN ASSEMBLY 160
MONITORING YOUR PLAN 161
THE REAL WORK 162

THE AFTERWORD 163

INDEX 164

ORDER FORMS 171

About The Author

Joe Wolosz has worked for some of the most innovative hotel companies in regard to sales and marketing. From industry leader Hyatt Hotels and Resorts to the cutting edge upstart The Kimpton Group, Wolosz has joined forces to bring hospitality sales to the 21st century. With an ever-decreasing sales budget, Wolosz took to innovative approaches to get "heads in beds", raise average rates and *impact the bottom line*.

His university education took him to southern California to earn a Bachelor of Science degree in Hotel and Restaurant Management at California Polytechnic University, Pomona. The university is considered by the hospitality industry as a leader on the west coast.

Presently Wolosz is deftly assisting in the real estate transactions of hotels, motels and other lodging properties in the role of broker. Talking with many of the smaller property owners, Wolosz became aware of the glaring absence of any text that was focused on the marketing of a small property with little or no budget. In the creation of Hotel and Motel Sales, Marketing and Promotion, Wolosz has stripped down the elaborate marketing tactics of the big hotel companies and recreated them for the small property owner/operator or manager.

Additionally, Wolosz teaches Hospitality Sales and Marketing, Front Office, Quality Management and Convention Management, among other American Hotel & Motel Association courses, at the Hospitality Management Training Institute in downtown San Francisco. He speaks at various functions on the topics of yield management, marketing and promotion.

Wolosz presently works with National Hotel and Motel Brokers and lives in San Francisco, California. He can be reached by telephone at 415-292-5639 or e-mail at corridor@slip.net.

Acknowledgment

It would be impossible to give credit to all sources that I consulted in the preparation of this book. The list would exhaust the space available. The primary contributor would undoubtedly be the California Polytechnic University, Pomona and their dedication to education at their School of Hotel and Restaurant Management, as well as Maxine and Joe Wolosz, my parents, whose support has been invaluable.

There are scores of people who aided in the completion of this text, willingly contributing their time and effort. Information and support were contributed by Joe Lambert, Dayna Zietlin, Jim Morgan, Neal and Nita Patel, Tarun Kapoor, Sandy Kapoor, Robert Kemper, Chip Conely, Kerry Flowers, Lynda Backman, Lychee Chiu, David George, Sherri Sands, Jeanette Trtanj, Jai Sharma, Bender Purewall, Roxanne McDermott, Cynthia Hiponia, Kevin Crosby, Rhonda Paige, Michael Incorvaia, Peter Gamez, John Banta, Hal Gayden, Robb Curry (and his newborn son), Cheryl Pickerell, Darin Carnie, Gloria Ware, Traci Baily, John Figone, Michael Zaleski, Ian Blackburn, Mark Schwass, Barb Bogdanski, Sandra Powell, Sherris Goodwin, Leonie Spencer, Dave Groff, Matt Gray, Gary Hamilton, Robert Palmer, Robert Small, and my university Hotel Sales and Marketing professor Ms. Margie Jones (you didn't know what impact you had on me).

I extend a big thank you to them all. I hope they will take pride in being part of this finished product.

Warning–Disclaimer

This book is sold as an aid for the marketing and promotion of lodging properties. This book does not provide — nor is it a substitute for — legal, accounting or professional advice. If such assistance is needed it is suggested to seek the services of a professional.

This book is not a comprehensive text on the subject matter. It is not a reprint of all the information available to the author and publisher on the subject. This book is meant as strictly a supplement to all the other texts available on the topics of hotels, motels, sales, marketing, promotion and any other subject highlighted in this book.

Sales, marketing and promotion is not a substitute for providing a quality product, but merely a means of attracting interest to, and obtaining a commitment to use, your product. For many with a quality product, a sales and marketing strategy is a way to match their services to the needs of others.

The author and publisher have made every effort to create a book that is as complete, accurate and relevant as possible. It is possible, however, that there could be mistakes. These mistakes can be not only typographical but also in the content. Because of this it is recommended that this book be only used as a guide in hotel and motel sales, marketing and promotion. The information included is only as current as the printing date.

This book is sold with the purpose to entertain and educate. The author and Infinite Corridor Publishing accepts no liability nor responsibility for any loss or damage to any person or entity, alleged or caused, whether it be directly or indirectly, because of the information contained in the text and illustrations of this book.

If you do not wish to be bound by the above, you may return this book to the publisher for a full refund.

Chapter 1 Welcome

Compelling Reasons to Create a Plan

Competition in the lodging industry has become heavy this past decade and all indicators point to an escalating battle vying for reservations at an acceptable rate. If you can't compete, you will ultimately be pushed out; only the smart survive. With this competitive environment in mind, it stands to reason that every property welcomes any increase in occupancy, rate and overall revenue. A dramatic increase is preferred. There is an established formula to propel a property to revenue success; a well designed Sales and Marketing Plan suited specifically for each property.

> The beginning is half of every action. — Greek Proverb

But many operators feel that the efforts to overcome obstacles standing in the way of functionally promoting their property are greater than the probable result. These obstacles may seem insurmountable. History may have taught them that marketing and sales are areas where they can easily spin their wheels, spend enormous sums of money and see little result. In the end, they may eschew marketing spending and accept the status quo because they fear making costly promotion and advertising mistakes. There have been few resources that a smaller, and perhaps an economically challenged, property could consult for help. Most information on hospitality sales and marketing is geared toward larger resort and city center properties with many amenities and big budgets. This book is meant for the rest of us.

This book will help you separate what can impact your bottom line dollars and what will only fill the pockets of someone else. It is this book's aim to steer you clear of these impediments and set you on your way to increasing your occupancy, rate and revenue. New paths in hospitality marketing will be presented for you to pursue. While you may not absorb all the items put forth in one reading, they will yield perspective and insight as you gain familiarity with the process of creating the Sales and Marketing Plan.

> **Business is a college more exacting than any of the schools and universities.** — Thomas Edison

Later, you will undoubtedly be referring to this book again and again. It is advised however that you read it through once from cover to cover. It is necessary to perform certain tasks and calculations along the way that will bring you closer to a final Sales and Marketing Plan. They follow a logical sequence that lend to reading it beginning to end.

Trends Affecting the Lodging Industry

The hospitality industry has experienced some dramatic changes over the past decade. The over-building in the eighties, the creation of the mega-resort (where you can "swim with the dolphins"), the recession during the early nineties and the improved health of the hospitality industry only begin to illustrate the dynamic climate in which we live. This is only a sample of what is to come. Today the lodging operator is faced with stronger and smarter competition through consolidations, the entrance of new competition as a result of the growing legalization of gambling, and hotel industry leaders carving up markets through brand segmentation.

The trend of consolidation is demonstrated daily as we read about United States budget chain Motel 6 purchased by French company Accor, Days Inn joining the family at Holiday Franchise Systems, Holiday Inn acquired by Bass PLC of London and as Hilton pulls its domestic and international properties together. Consolidation offers these companies many benefits including increased purchasing power, synergistic sales and marketing effort, reduced expenses as they allocate them over a greater number of properties and increased brand recognition.

Forms of legalized gambling are spreading across the United States. With the construction of additional gaming venues comes an increase in tourism as tourist destinations multiply. Gaming has become a way to create a destination where there would not be a demand otherwise. Before casinos, Las Vegas was a small roadside town, hardly a tourist destination. But that is not to say that the increase in tourists is in direct proportion with the increase in available guest rooms. All properties must compete for travelers and an increase in *destination* choices may only spread the available traveler pool a little thinner. Another concern is the increase in *lodging* choices once a destination decision has been made by the traveler. Any increase in room construction forces operators to become fierce in the competition for guests.

The hotel and motel industry has always segmented itself into three categories; the budget segment, the mid-priced segment and the luxury segment. Recently the hotel chains have been attempting to generate greater loyalty through brand awareness by creating "brands" of their products. A fine example is Holiday Inn whose brands now include, in ascending order; Holiday Inn Express, Holiday Inn, Holiday Inn Select and Crown Plaza by Holiday Inn. Marriott also has done well with its Courtyard by Marriott, Residence Inn, Fairfield Inn and Marriott properties.

These trends can affect the distribution of available travelers and are, for the most part, out of *your* control. They only illustrate the importance of remaining competitive. There are trends in the lodging industry – such as computers and technology, the aging of the baby boomer population, the rise of ecotourism and the shifts in the average American household – that you can analyze and put to use in increasing the effectiveness of your marketing effort.

Computers have become indispensable in the allocation of guest rooms, especially for larger hotel chains with central reservations networks. These computer systems not only allow the employees on property to book a reservation but also allows the affiliation – such as Best Western – to check availability. Even for a property without any chain or network affiliation a computerized reservations system will allow the property to quickly track occupancy, rate and revenue per available room (revPAR) as well as maintain a quality database with valuable information. A computer can aid in direct mail sales efforts, generating personalized letters to a large group of people, maintain standardized responses to various situations and follow up on key contacts.

The aging of the baby boomer population is of significant importance to the lodging and tourism industry. The population of people entering retirement and semi-retirement is increasing at a dramatic pace as this generation matures. This segment of the population is attractive because it has the available time to travel and many have the disposable income.

Ecotourism is a word that we are hearing more and more. It generally points to some type of travel that is in harmony with nature; whether you enjoy a sojourn to a remote region and conduct yourself without harming the environment or experiencing a "green room" in a city hotel. A green room is a guest room that is environmentally friendly through amenities made of recycled products, reduced services such as laundering, and cleaned with environmentally responsible products, among other things.

What is deemed the American household has undergone extensive changes. More women are working today and many are choosing not to marry or to marry later in life. Many are having children later as well. These factors point to an increase in the segment of single adults who have increased freedom and money for travel. Of those that do marry, many create two-income families with both partners in the work force. While this may cut down on the amount of time they have to travel, they are still opting to have children later. With this in mind and their increased income they are able to take shorter vacations more often throughout the year.

The Marketing Plan

By going through the process of identifying markets that you can accommodate and how you can attract them you are better able to focus your undertaking with clarity and precision. Your research can uncover opportunities in your existing markets and show you some markets that you may want to pursue. The research will also highlight markets that are unsuitable or that you may want to steer clear. The final plan will list your property's objectives, identify the necessary responsibilities and assign the appropriate person to each task. This plan will become a constant source of valuable information and guidance, helping you to use your resources economically to generate the greatest result.

Creating a marketing plan will force you to think to the future, anticipate obstacles, identify tactics and use your time and energies efficiently. Having the knowledge that the process of creating the plan gives will put you in a powerful position. You will *act* rather than *react* and your decisions will be informed ones. Assembling a quality Sales and Marketing Plan requires working through ten steps. These ten steps are the body of this book:

- Analysis of your property,
- Analysis of your competition,
- Analysis of the market,
- Identifying target markets,
- Orientating the property's position,
- Creating a promotional strategy,
- Determining objectives,
- Creating an action plan,
- Determining a budget, and
- Monitoring and constantly evaluating the effectiveness of the Sales and Marketing Plan.

Adopt the Spirit of the Entrepreneur

Regardless of whether you actually own the lodging property in question, it is well advised to think, act and react as an entrepreneur. Entrepreneurs break from the flock and forge new successes. They radiate vitality and excellence. They are innovators and greet innovation. *They are excited!* But most importantly entrepreneurs are persistent; never giving up. By constantly looking for ways to improve your property, service and amenities you will also give diligent thought and pursuit to better and more effective ways to sell and market you hotel or motel. Pay close attention to the trends that are now present in the lodging industry. Find ways to use them to your advantage. Cultivate the *intensity* that is the hallmark of entrepreneurs. And if you do own the facility then you will want to capitalize on your entrepreneurial drive.

Now is the Time to Take Action

Are you restless or bored? Is your property not a source of the income you had expected? Do you feel that, given the proper tools, or pointed in the right direction, that your facility can meet with higher occupancies and better rates? Maybe you are just a little unsure of what approach to take and what to expect from the different options available. If you

> **It is later than you think. — Chinese Proverb**

do have these feelings of restlessness, and even anxiety, use them. Channel them to drive you to study this book and its techniques. Many university hotel programs teach that any lodging property (or food and beverage outlet) *can be successful* but that it is entirely management's (owner's) responsibility and that any non-success — a poor employee for instance — is a reflection of that management. Think about that for a minute. **Any property can be successful.** Now, it may require repositioning, such as remodeling so that you can target a different market or contracting tour buses to stop by as they drive cross country or calling all the trucking companies to accommodate their divers. The spirit of the entrepreneur that built this country, and has been inspiration for people around the world, will find a way to make any property work. It takes effort, some more than others but effort all the same. Once you can face and accept these truths, then can you focus your effort with laser precision to achieve the revenue goals you plan. This book will help you with arriving at a detailed and focused Sales and Marketing Plan and give you techniques that you may implement to make your plan's objectives a reality.

Chapter 1
Welcome

Without an established plan, the marketing and promotion of a lodging property can be a daunting task. This seems especially true in today's hospitality business world where it may feel like an operator has to fight for every guest room booked. The operator may feel that he or she is going in many different directions at once with little to show for the effort. The key is to call "time out" and draw up a plan that is founded in fact and reality. This will be your lean and mean Sales and Marketing Plan.

Very few companies can show stellar income reports by sitting back and waiting for business to come to them. Even if some can, the laws of the growth cycle make certain that this approach cannot be effective forever. Eventually they will pass the maturity phase and enter into decline. No longer is it possible for a lodging property to be successful by offering clean rooms alone. Today, you must

> **When you work for yourself, you become an innovator or you don't eat.**
> **— J. W. Marriott**

find a way to ensure that your property will receive a steady flow of guests. To do this, you, as an operator, must have a working knowledge of sales and marketing and put that knowledge to active use.

In addition to the preparation, time and patience of drafting the plan, it also takes hard work to carry out the action steps that you have outlined. Fortunately, with a well thought out Sales and Marketing Plan, you can move ahead each day with confidence that you will accomplish the necessary tasks to achieve your stated revenue, occupancy and rate goals. Thomas Edison once said, "Opportunity is missed by most because it is dressed in overalls and looks like work". However, seldom is work a chore when the fruits of your labor make evident the economy of your action. There are many opportunities that you can exploit to fill your guest rooms. This book will start you off.

What You Need To Know To Begin

This book will take you through many of the different marketing, promotion and sales ideas that are used in the industry. In preparing this book, I have taken techniques used by larger hotel companies, like Hyatt and Sheraton, and distilled the principles so that it can be applicable to a smaller property. Some ideas have come from working with smaller, independent properties. There are others that come from sales and marketing techniques used by other industries that lodging properties would be wise to adopt. You most likely will think of others that can apply to your property. If you do, I'd like to hear of them. My phone, fax and e-mail are all listed in the back of the book. To get the most out of your reading, you are encouraged to adopt the following three points.

Use a yellow highlighter. This book is not a novel and should not, in any way, be read like one. This is a guide and a text book. It is meant to be written in, dog-eared and underlined. Keep a yellow highlighter with it at all times. The purpose is to increase revenue, not to keep the book looking like new. Do not be gentle, it can withstand rough use.

Keep an open mind. Your property is indeed unique. However, if you find that a particular technique or tactic does not seem to fit your property, try to think of ways that you can adapt it. Average people will give reasons why an idea will not work for them. Great people will look to find all the ways they can adjust an idea so they can apply it to their circumstance. Exceptional people will go one step further and come up with other ideas of their own to replace ones, that for some reason, cannot apply. Shoot for exceptional.

Use this book as a catalyst to grow ideas of your own. Nobody knows your property better than you. Develop new ways to generate business that will propel you to achieve the revenue, growth and position your property deserves.

Creating a Sales and Marketing Plan is not necessarily difficult, but it does demand a considerable amount of research and thought. A solid marketing plan will not fail because there was too much time invested in the planning, but many have taken a downward spiral because of too little. When you are finished with the plan, you will be pleased with your work, secure in the fact that you will be moving in a positive and results oriented direction.

> **Whether you think you can or think you can't, you're right. — Henry Ford**

If you are involved with the marketing of a small property and also work in an operations capacity, i.e. accounting, housekeeping, or front desk, you will want to note a major difference between other departments and the Sales and Marketing department. Every department's goal should be to increase profits. Most will attempt to achieve this through *cost containment*. However, the Sales and Marketing department focuses on increasing profits by *increasing revenue*. The other department that would come close is Reservations. As they take calls they have the opportunity to close the sale and to up-sell. Any property can be good at both cost containment and increasing revenue. These pages will help you with the latter.

Marketing in the hospitality industry differs from most other industries and has its own challenges. There is an *intangibility* to overcome when selling guest rooms. When we talk about selling guest rooms, we are not actually selling the room but rather the use of the guest room. Because it is a service, after a guest checks out and leaves the property, he or she will not have anything tangible to take home with them that they can show in exchange for the money spent. Hospitality shares this aspect with other service industries. But it is not only a service but also *100% perishable.* Meaning that if you have a 50 room property and sell 45 rooms one night, the next day you will only have 50 rooms that you can try to sell. You cannot gain the five rooms that went unused the previous night. In this light, you can see how imperative it is to maximize every opportunity you have to sell those guest rooms. A final challenge is that there is no separation between the production of the service and its consumption. It is simultaneous in the sense that a guest enjoys the services at the moment that they are being created. This *inseparability* is closely related to the challenge of intangibility.

Some Definitions Defined

Sales: Any direct action taken in which the objective is to effect the *sale (rental)* of a guest room or block of guest rooms. Selling is a direct effort to fill the property.

Marketing: Any action taken in which the objective is to effect *interest or inquiry* by a potential user of the guest rooms. Marketing is an indirect effort to fill the property.

User: Any individual or entity that has a need for guest rooms. Examples are individual travelers, travel agents, tour operators, meeting planners, companies and corporations.

Product: The lodging property. This is what the user is purchasing; the use of your hotel or motel.

Lodging industry marketing is researching room night demand, pinpointing available business and satisfying the need of potential business by the introduction and use of your property. This marketing should become an integral part of your life. It is the lifeblood of your property. It is what fills the guest room and gets the heads in your beds. It is being receptive to the demands of the market and satisfying them, creating a profit in turn. Even a relatively small operator can commit to learn more about its guests to provide a basis for a effective marketing plan. Can you say that you subscribe to this concept of marketing?

Research Methodology

There is a methodology to marketing research. As with eating a meal, the key to accomplishing the task at hand is to break it down into small, digestible bites. With a method set out on how to prepare for the marketing plan you will move smoothly and confidently through the process and less likely to leave anything out. Use the research methodology for each part of your analysis. An example is given to illustrate each point.

Define the challenge. Focus on what it is that you are looking to answer. Ask questions as to what solution you are seeking, such as, "How can I evaluate the quality of service offered at the hotel?"

Seek direction. Briefly investigate the task. What resources do you have available that point to a solution. Guest comment cards, letters to the management, polling the employees for their input, and "eaves dropping" in the lobby can point you in a direction.

Plan the investigation. This is what you will do and how will you go about doing it. An example is thinking of other ways you can get to the "pulse" of your service level. You may implement exit surveys of guests willing to talk before they leave or have an honest acquaintance give you feedback.

Collect all the information. Go about finding all the necessary and/or available data. Organize it. The format you use will depend on you or how it is suggested by this book for the different areas of research.

Give conclusions based on the data. This is where you take the data and put it into a useful form. What does it mean? Interpret and reach conclusions. This is a step that is often skimmed over. Some people feel that they have collected all the data and that it should speak for itself. The data in that form is not yet useful. You must interpret how the data relates to your situation. Perform if/then scenarios and give careful analysis to the different outcomes. Interpretation makes the data *meaningful* and meaningful data is what you need to put together a plan that can do nothing but generate the desired results.

How the Material is Organized in this Book

This book is designed so that you will conduct research and analysis and document your findings and conclusions as you progress. You will be doing far more than merely observing, you will be creating a study of your property in the marketplace. Keep all the work that you do together as you will need it all at the final chapter when you compile it as a meaningful Sales and Marketing Plan that is custom designed for your property. I suggest you acquire a three ring binder and keep all your research together.

This icon, ➡, is used throughout this book to indicate an area where you will be asked to complete something before you go forward. This book has been organized in a logical order of steps necessary to create your plan. Again, I strongly suggest that the first time you read through it you do so from beginning to end, completing each of the tasks put to you.

The studies in this book are set up for the creation of a Sales and Marketing Plan for one year, presumably beginning January 1. If you are reading this book to begin a plan earlier I suggest that you extend the plan to cover all the months till December 31st of the following year. If January 1st just past then you may want to cut the plan to just finish out that year.

Because the ideas presented in this book can be used for hotels, motels, bed and breakfasts, inns, hostels, lodges and whatever else can be dreamed up, I have opted for the all encompassing term *lodging property*. With a few exceptions you will find the term used throughout the book. Certain areas I will refer to a *hotel or motel*, understand that it is to add variety and take off the "technical edge." These terms are a general reference to all types of lodging properties.

On Your Mark...

Organizing your marketing effort will give you a whole new focus. It refreshes you with the feeling that your expended energies are being used in the most efficient and economical way. It cuts the fat, makes you lean and builds your endurance. Your property will have direction and purpose. But to decide on a direction for your property, you will want a clear understanding of your present situation. You must first create an analysis of your property. Continue your reading and write plenty of notes. Underline, highlight and come back for more. There is a lot to learn and even more to be gained. Enjoy the pursuit.

Chapter 2 Research: Making the Information Meaningful

Beginning Your Study

This chapter will take you on a very informative tour of your immediate market climate, both in terms of your property and those of your competition. In order to begin any marketing and promotion, you should give careful analysis of your current situation regarding these three areas:

> **Facts do not cease to exist because they are ignored.** — Aldous Huxley

- Your physical property,
- Your competition, and
- The market climate.

You must have a clear picture of all these in order to be successful in marketing your product as well as to have a standard to measure your success. The axiom holds true, "Knowledge is power!" Once these three items are understood and digested you are infinitely more prepared for the task at hand and you will have a method to realistically approach achieving your set forecast.

Analysis Of Your Property Occupancy, Rate and RevPAR.

Be ruthless, be honest and be brutal. In order for the appraisal of your property to be of any use you must remain unbiased. This is not the time to flatter yourself or pat yourself on the back, although that most certainly will come later. To get a firm idea of your market penetration you must consider the following:

- Your annual occupancy for last year,
- Your occupancy for each month last year,
- Your average daily rate (ADR) for last year, calculated annually,
- Your ADR calculated for each month last year,
- Your revenue per available room (revPAR), calculated for last year, and
- Your revPAR calculated for each month last year.

If you do not keep these records, resolve now that you will from here on out, and then go back through your records and daily receipts and calculate. Having this accurate information will quickly show you where there is room for improvement in rate and occupancy.

➡ If you do not have records of you occupancy, ADR and revPAR for the last 12 months, broken down by month, take the time to do it now. Write this information on a separate piece of paper and put it inside your three ring binder. Commit to a policy that you will do it continuously beginning now. If you are in the market for new front desk software, consider getting one that will calculate this information for you. This is also fantastic information to have on hand when it comes time to sell your property (I am talking about selling the real estate and business). Pull your *daily* receipts for the past year and calculate the following:

Your annual occupancy for last year, percentage.

$$\frac{total\ rooms\ sold\ last\ year}{number\ of\ units\ on\ your\ property \times 365} \times 100$$

Your occupancy for each month last year, percentage.

$$\frac{total\ rooms\ sold\ that\ month}{number\ of\ units\ on\ your\ property \times 30} \times 100$$

Your ADR for last year, calculated annually.

$$\frac{gross\ room\ receipts\ for\ that\ year *}{number\ of\ rooms\ sold\ that\ year}$$

Your ADR calculated for each month last year.

$$\frac{gross\ room\ receipts\ for\ the\ month *}{number\ of\ rooms\ sold\ that\ month}$$

*Not including occupancy tax.

Your revPAR, calculated for last year.

$$\frac{\text{gross room receipts for the year}}{\text{number of units on your property}**\times 365}$$

Your revPAR calculated for each month last year.

$$\frac{\text{gross room receipts for the year}}{\text{number of units on your property}**\times 30}$$

✶✶The revPAR calculations are assuming you do not have any units out of order due to renovations or repairs. If this were the case then the denominator (the bottom half of the equation) would read "number of rentable units for the year" or "number of rentable units for the month".

Remember yearly occupancy and ADR is not their monthly sums divided by 12. If you only sold 50 rooms in December for $100 each, your ADR would be $100. Compared to the 700 rooms you sold in September at an ADR of $60, your revenue is much greater in September but your ADR is lower. You can see the possibility for error. Take the time to generate accurate data, otherwise the information will not be useful, even if sometimes it would seem so. Even if it seems to be coming "close enough" remember a stopped clock is still right twice a day. After you have completed, create tables similar to the ones that follow, eliminating the word *specimen*, and fill in your figures.

Your annual occupancy for last year:

Year	Occupancy
199_ *specimen*	*specimen*

Your occupancy for each month:

Month	Occupancy	Month	Occupancy
January	*specimen*	**February**	
March		**April**	
May		**June**	
July		**August**	
September		**October**	
November		**December**	

Your ADR for last year:

Year	ADR
199_ *specimen*	*specimen*

Your ADR calculated for each month:

Month	ADR	Month	ADR
January	*specimen*	**February**	
March		**April**	
May		**June**	
July		**August**	
September		**October**	
November		**December**	

Your revPAR, calculated for last year:

Year	revPAR
199_ *specimen*	*specimen*

Your revPAR calculated for each month:

Month	revPAR	Month	revPAR
January	*specimen*	**February**	
March		**April**	
May		**June**	
July		**August**	
September		**October**	
November		**December**	

Looking to the Future Through the Use of Yield Management

In the not-too-distant past, a lodging property's performance was measured either by occupancy or ADR. However, these numbers on their own tell us very little. Take into consideration a hotel that has a very high occupancy *because* of its low room rates. The occupancy figure may look attractive, but compared with the end result – the overall revenue produced – it may not be attractive at all. The converse is also true; a hotel may have an ADR of $250 last night, but they only rented the one suite, making the total revenue for the evening only $250.

A yield statistic takes into account the relationship between ADR and occupancy, and represents the relationship as a single statistic, or percentage.

Whereas in the past lodging properties focused their effort on maximizing occupancies, sometimes at all costs, today the focus is on maximizing revenue. We can do this by using **yield management**.

> Yield management: Maximizing revenue (occupancy and rate) through the use of historical forecasting to assign rate criteria to dates. This is used in the decision process to take, turn away or move an individual's or group's reservation.

The airline industry was the pioneer in using yield management. It is understood by most that the travelers on any particular flight may have paid any number of rates, often with a variance of hundreds of, or even over a thousand, dollars. We are all familiar with the lower rate for the Saturday stay over or the twenty-one day advance purchase. They do this to *maximize the revenue* they earn. Essentially, you will want to take a lead from the airline industry and implement a yield management system. To do this you must shift your focus as appropriate. The foundation of this plan is to focus on maximizing rates over **high demand periods** and focus on maximizing occupancies over **low demand, or need, periods**, and moving business from your high demand periods into your **shoulder periods**.

> High demand periods: Dates when occupancies for your property are high. Business is good. Also called *peak periods*.
>
> Need periods: Dates when occupancies for your property are low. You need business. Also called *valley periods*.
>
> Shoulder periods: Dates that fall between large blocks of high demand periods and need periods. An example is a property that has historically busy summers and slow winters would have the months of October and April as the shoulder periods. They are excellent periods on which to focus to increase business.

You can adopt this revenue managing concept to your efficient operation with a simple calendar. History repeats itself. With your history mapped out you can see the hills and valleys identifying high demand periods, need periods and shoulder periods. You will want to map out your *history* so that you can forecast your *future*.

➲Take a large calendar for the last 12 months. Using the previous formulas, adapt them to calculate the occupancy and ADR for *each day*. Write these figures into the appropriate calendar day. This is your **history**.

On another calendar for the coming 12 months, create your **forecast** using the date as your primary reference from the history calendar. You first consideration will be to fill in the date specific events. These are happenings that will bring in travelers that will impact your property. If the Clam Festival held last year on May 25th was a success in filling your guest rooms, you will want to know when it will be this year. If the festival will fall on May 23rd, then fill out your calendar accordingly. After all the planned events are filled in you will want to switch your focus to the *day* as opposed to the actual *date* of your history calendar because most travel patterns are affected by the *day* of the week. This exercise will require a bit of intuition and educated guess work to fill in a projected occupancy for each day. Do your best and use your instincts. Contact your local Chamber of Commerce and the Convention and Visitors' Bureau to give you a calendar of upcoming events to use on this project.

Occupancy drives rate. If occupancies are forecasted to be high, then the rates you quote will be high and you may opt to turn away lower rated business or move it into need periods and shoulder periods. Looking at your future calendar you can see your high demand dates. The available rooms you have over these dates are valuable and should be sold accordingly. You will mark each of these days with the letter **A** (see the following exercise). This is your highest rate code and it is reserved for the dates that you will sell out. You are quoting **rack rates** over these dates.

> Rack rate: Your highest published rate for a particular room.

> ➲Assign rate codes to each date. This will let your staff know which rates are not available and the proper rate to quote, **A** being rack rate only, **B** being 10% discount off of rack up to rack rate, and so on. You should update these codes as room availability shifts, once a week at least, and more frequent for dates two weeks out or less if business is volatile. All who answer the reservations line are able to quote the same rate and this will help to avoid the guest dissatisfaction associated with rate inconsistencies.

If you have a history of selling out the third week of August and someone calls in January for these dates, you can refer to your forecast and know to quote rack rate. If they decide not to book you can feel certain that the closer you get to these dates your property will eventually fill at the higher rate.

Another benefit is you can identify need and shoulder periods and focus your effort to fill them. With that same caller your effort can go something like this, "The rate for those dates is $75 a night, are your dates flexible?" If they answer yes, tell them about the economical offering the following week when your property is forecasted to be slow. By moving business this way you are able to fill revenue holes and work on the need periods every time someone calls. Now you are in control of your room inventory and taking the steps to fill your rooms.

The Yield Statistic

In the same way that you will want to track your occupancy and ADR, you will also want to track your yield. As mentioned earlier, the numbers for occupancy or ADR mean very little as they stand alone. It is only in relation to one another that they give any meaningful information. The yield statistic is a single figure used to represent the health of a property. It takes into consideration rates and occupancy and can be calculated as follows:

$$Yield\ statistic = \frac{Actual\ rooms\ revenue}{Potential\ rooms\ revenue}$$

To calculate your yield for a particular night you will take the actual revenue received and divide it by your potential. Your potential is the revenue received *if you sold every room (100% occupancy) on your property and you sold each of them at their rack rate.* This is the most you can make in one night. A simple example would be a 50 unit property with a rack rate for all rooms of $75. The potential rooms revenue for this property would be 50 rooms times $75, or $3,750. If the property's occupancy was 70% and the ADR was $59.70, then you could calculate the yield statistic as follows:

$$\text{Yield statistic} = \frac{(50 \text{ rooms} \times 70\%) \times \$59.70}{\$3,750}$$

$$\text{Yield statistic} = \frac{35 \text{ rooms} \times \$59.70}{\$3,750}$$

$$\text{Yield statistic} = \frac{\$2,089.50}{\$3,750}$$

$$\text{Yield statistic} = 56\%$$

➡ Calculate your yield statistic for last year. As you use the yield statistic it will take on more meaning. Just as when you begin tracking the statistics of your favorite ball player, the statistics mean more when you are following it for a while and compare it with the past performance and that of the other players, or in your case, the competition.

Exploring Your Property Through Quantitative and Qualitative Analysis.

Performing quantitative and qualitative analysis brings your focus from your production to your offering. What do you bring to the marketplace? What you want to do is to create an analytical picture of who and what your property is. With this information you can match available markets to your product and target those markets. Now that you have a firm grasp of your occupancy, rate, revPAR situation and yield statistic, you need to take stock of your physical property in both **quantitative** and **qualitative** terms.

> Quantitative: Tangible terms with definite answers. Objective in nature. Examples are number of rooms, room configuration, pool, mini-bars, amenities offered and parking.
>
> Qualitative: Harder to assign a value. Subjective in nature. Examples are level of service and cleanliness, popularity of your area and location and quality of your property.

The quantitative part is fairly simple to assess. It covers all the things that can be identified the same way by any reasonable person; the answers are objective. Items to consider:

- Number of rooms,
- Room configuration,
- Location,
- Amenities offered,
- Age of building,
- Rates,
- Meeting space (size, configuration),
- Food and beverage (offered?),
- Gross revenues,
- Expenses,
- Packages offered, and
- Check in and check out times.

Things that are qualitative in nature are equally as important to determine, however they may prove to be much more difficult to positively identify and assign a value. Items like *level of service* mean different things to different people. The same with *cleanliness* and *value*. Keep in mind travelers are more sophisticated and they have a base expectation for these things. Simply meeting their expectations does nothing more for them than does finding a mirror in the bathroom; it is exactly what was expected for the price paid. Be honest with your evaluation of things like service, quality and value. You don't want to cheat yourself if you have room for improvement. For future use, keep in mind that a good way to ensure repeat business is to always exceed guests' expectations.

I point this out so you are careful not to overstate your stance on these qualitative points. This is not a contest. Be brutally honest with yourself about your product. It is only from a platform grounded in reality that you can build an effective marketing plan and sales effort.

Qualitative items are subjective. Consider having your staff and friends help you assign a value to these items. You can use the information that they give to create a realistic analysis. Points to consider:

- Level of service,
- Level of cleanliness,
- Perceived value,
- Popularity of location,
- Aesthetic appeal,
- Reputation, and
- Public's perception of your property.

Analysis of the Competition

If you are isolated from other properties – you are alone in your market – then your physical property and amenities are important to a much lesser degree. These things only take their relevance when held in comparison to the offerings of your competitors. This can also hold true when comparing amenities; if you do not offer room service, it will not be viewed as a limitation if no other property in your area offers it. You can see the importance of building your competitive knowledge.

You will want to know as much about your competition as you do about your own property. This may be asking a lot and you don't want to get bogged down in the planning phase, so if it seems appropriate, choose those properties that you compete with most frequently. The properties you choose will be your **competitive set**.

> Competitive set: A group of lodging properties that have been identified as your direct competition.

You will create compact dossiers on each of these properties and continually update the information that you have on them.

In choosing the properties for the competitive set ask yourself, "Do I ever loose business to that property?" If a property's rate is much higher or lower than yours then it is most likely not in direct competition. Keep in mind you may compete with different properties for different markets. You may loose corporate business to

Hotel ABC down the street and loose government business to Motel XYZ.

Take the time to visit each of these properties personally. Get to know the owner or manager. They can refer business to you when they are sold out. Have them give you a tour of their property. Collect the same quantitative and qualitative data as you did with your property. If you have the opportunity, stay the night at these properties.

> ➲Prepare a competitive analysis, see example. Have a separate sheet of paper for each property including your own. List all the quantitative and qualitative data you collected. Include strengths and weaknesses. You will use these in selling against your competition. Set up this sheet in whatever format feels most comfortable.

You have to know the competition to stay ahead of them. If you are going to compete for the same business, you have to know what they are offering. A guest can only stay at one property at a time. If they are comparison shopping you will have a difficult time steering them into your property with out a working knowledge of all the other offerings. This competitive analysis may also show you markets that are being served by your competitor that can also benefit from your property. Also, someday business may be so good that your will want to own another property in your area. You will have a better idea of who to pick up and already have most of the marketing plan finished!

If you are able to gather accurate data on all the properties in your competitive set regarding their occupancy and number of available rooms that they have during the year (most likely the number of rooms they have times 365, unless some were out of commission due to renovations and repairs) then you will be able to calculate **market share** and **fair share** for each property including your own.

$$market\ share = \frac{individual\ property\ room\ nights\ sold}{total\ market\ room\ nights\ sold} \times 100$$

$$fair\ share = \frac{individual\ property\ available\ room\ nights}{total\ market\ available\ room\ nights} \times 100$$

The denominator refers to all the guest rooms in your area (yours and your competitor's) either sold or available. Market share will show you the percentage each property is actually reaping of the total incoming guest market. Fair share is a straight line calculation that shows you what percentage *should be* received by each property based solely on dividing up the incoming guest base by the available number of rooms.

> ➡After you have decided on your competitive set, monitor them closely so you can get an idea of total yearly demand for rooms for all the properties of the set including your own. You can then monitor *your property's* current penetration of that demand. Attempt to calculate market share and fair share for your competitive set and your own property. Take it a step further and break it down by market segment (more on this later). Note any anticipated or expected changes in room supply (a

property adding units or closing down) and changes in demand. Give reasons for these demand changes. This information will prove invaluable when locating areas to improve market penetration.

The Marketing Mix

The marketing mix consists of four variables that affect the purchase decision of a potential user. They are often referred to as the "four P's" called product, promotion, place and price. They are observed by most industries in their marketing efforts. However, because of the unique challenges that are involved with marketing and selling guest rooms; intangibility, perishability and inseparability, we must look at the four P's with an unconventional eye.

Product in this case would also refer to the services offered. In addition to the use of the guest room, your property is also offering services such as housekeeping and concierge.

Promotion refers to the way your property communicates its offering to the targeted market.

Place would usually refer to the manner in which the product is offered to the consumer. With a lodging property, the guest actually comes to the property to use the product/service. While the guest must actually come to the property's address to use the product, you can bring the property to a guest in a virtual sense in that the reservation channels are brought to them or made readily accessible. Channels to consider can include your toll free reservations line, travel agents cr a web site.

Price is the rate you attach to your offering. The approach to pricing and its structure will be covered in chapter three.

Analysis of the Market

In the past, hoteliers spent their marketing dollars trying to reach everyone, all the time. But marketing for lodging properties has grown up a bit. Owners and operators are focusing their efforts with **niche marketing**.

> Niche marketing: Focusing marketing efforts to a specific segment of the population.

You will want to give careful consideration to the analysis of markets for two reasons; first, your sales effort will never be a proven success if your markets have not been selected consciously and intelligently, and second, armed with the information from your competitive analysis, you will select market sources best suited for you offering with the least competition.

There are many market segments to consider when promoting your property. Within each of these segments you will find the possibility of both **group** and **individual** business.

> Group business: Considered by most in the industry to be at least five rooms per night from one source. Larger hotels may

require at least ten rooms per night for the source to be considered for a group rate.

Individual business: Considered by most in the industry to be anything that does not fall under group business. This would include any **volume accounts**.

Volume accounts: Any source that offers your property a large amount of room nights spread out over the year. It is primarily individual business. Your property may receive a few room nights a month from this source.

It is good to have a working knowledge of how each segment is defined. There are idiosyncrasies particular to each and some require you to take on a different personality when dealing with them. The following is prepared to help you seek out and identify these markets. The social, military, educational, religious and fraternal markets together are often referred to as **SMERF** business because of the acronym that their names creates.

- Social,
- Military,
- Educational,
- Religious,
- Fraternal,
- Tour & Travel,
- Government,
- Corporate, and
- Association.

Social. All wedding, reunion and "get together" room blocks. Most of this business will come from your own backyard. Usually people in your community have invited others to come into your area. Capturing this business requires you to promote your property to local residents.

Military. Most often placed with the government category because it usually requires the government *per diem* rate (see definition under **Government**). These travelers may come from any branch of the armed services.

Educational. Colleges, universities and schools in your area can be a great source of business. Think of the lecturers, lecture attendees, parents of students, their friends and traveling teachers. The list is long.

Religious. The churches, temples, mosques and other places of worship frequently have speakers, clergy and others visit. There may also be people coming from out of town to attend a religious event.

Fraternal. Think of the Kiwanis, Rotary, Lions, Masons, Altrusa and the Daughters of the American Revolution. These organizations and many others have multiple events and invariably need guest rooms. Many meet once a month and can give steady, repeat business.

Tour & Travel. Sometimes referred to as *wholesale* business. It is extremely rate and location driven. Much of this business is in group form, but many **tour operators** offer **fly/drive packages** or other packages individuals can purchase. This market is rather complex in its appropriate terms and definitions, however the following should prove helpful.

> Tour operator: A company that negotiates preferred rates with hotels, airlines, rental cars, etc. in advance and resells them as a package to the end consumer at a marked up price. The end price is usually still at a lower price than the consumer will pay if he or she put the package together themselves. The tour operator sends a representative with the group to facilitate the trip.
>
> Fly/drive packages: Individual packages wholesalers or tour operators put together to be sold primarily through travel agencies. They include air transportation and car rental. This offers one stop shopping for the travel agent and the consumer.

Tour operators and wholesalers negotiate rates with lodging properties once a year. Because of the volume of business they hope to place at your property, they require a substantial discounted rate, often at 50% of your rack rate, or even less. If you are involved with a tour operator you will have the benefit of being included in their brochures and collateral as well as having their sales staff selling your property. Tour operators generally book three types of business.

> FIT: Read as F-I-T. Stands for foreign individual traveler or free independent traveler. This included fly/drive packages and other individual packages. The bulk

of these guests are from outside the United States.

Series group business: A series of separate yet similar groups throughout the year. Ordinarily they will require you to take all or most of the dates proposed. They will send your property a list of desired dates after they have negotiated a group rate with your property. Sometimes they will want a further discount in rate in exchange for placing the series at your property.

Ad hoc group business: This is the area in which they primarily use your negotiated rate, although there are properties who will only use the negotiated rate for any and all business form a tour operator. Ad hoc groups are the random groups for which the operator seeks availability at your property. Sometimes a third party has asked the tour operator to organize the group for them.

Government. The state and federal government have employees that travel. Both have set up **per diem rates** for different areas.

Per diem rates: Latin term meaning 'for or by the day.' This is their daily allowance and tells them how much they are allowed to spend on lodging. This gives them the autonomy to choose whichever property can accommodate the rate.

An example is that at press time, California state per diem for one night's lodging for the city of San Francisco was $96 and federal per diem for San Francisco was $113. Rack rates for many properties in the same city are over $200. If you do not know the per diem rates for your area you can call any local government agency and speak to someone who handles travel (it is a good idea to know this person anyway). If you area able to offer this rate, there maybe a world of business for your property.

Corporate. Look around your immediate area and take note of all the businesses there. Some of these businesses have people traveling to your area to visit them. Corporate business encompasses all travelers coming to stay in your area to conduct business.

Association. If you can think of a reason for people to get together then there will probably be an association for it. Most of these associations are headquartered in Washington DC. The most well known form of business that associations are responsible for is convention business. Depending on the size of the group they can use a local convention center or hold their convention at a hotel. Most small property operators cannot accommodate association convention business. However, you can position yourself to catch overflow when the host hotel can no longer accommodate.

Associations have many other types of meetings throughout the year that may be viable for your property. Board meetings, committee meetings, seminars and workshops are all used by associations.

The right association contact can bring in some less publicized room night and meeting business.

➡Create a pie chart of the various markets that you currently are catering and soliciting. To the best of your ability assign percentages of the pie to the different markets. Go through last year's daily receipts if you must and organize into the different categories outlined previously; SMERF, tour and travel, government, corporate, and association. By putting this into pie chart form you can see at a glance the possibilities for new markets to go after or existing markets that you want to exploit further. Remember corporate rates are usually higher than government, leisure travelers usually stay on Friday and Saturday night and tour and travel groups need your lowest rate in exchange for volume business. With all this in mind, draft a proposal pie chart for how you would like to see the market mix for your property. Break it into desired percentages; i.e. 40% corporate business, 10% government, 30% SMERF, and 20% tour and travel. You will refer to this and possibly fine tune it as you create your objectives, strategies and tactics in chapter seven.

Chapter 3 Identifying and Selecting Your Target Markets

Sources of Business

By focusing on the types of market segments, you may be thinking of different sources of new business or the possibility of getting additional room nights from existing people who use your property.

Your Chamber of Commerce is indispensable in locating new sources of business. You must be a member, but membership alone wont bring much business. You have to get involved and network. Marketing and promotion is not a spectator sport. The Chamber is a great resource to find out about a company that may be thinking of relocating in the area. This company will need guest rooms at the beginning while they are considering your area as will as while they are setting up operations. The first place they will contact is the Chamber of Commerce.

The Chamber wants to be as helpful as possible to lure new companies to the area. If you are a member they will welcome your brochures and your assurance you will take special care of anyone they send you. If companies are scouting out your area then they will probably need to stay overnight. You might even want to offer your Chamber a VIP package since they are trying to impress potential community investors. Offering a room upgrade and a special amenity will certainly be welcomed.

The Chamber is also an excellent place to network with other business leaders in the community. Attend the functions they have planned and flex your networking skills. Try to get to know all the people who work there. Leave some of your brochures for the members' business rack. This will help keep your property in front of their minds.

Many cities, towns and areas have Visitors' Centers or Tourist Welcome Centers. Set yourself apart from other properties; get out and meet the people who work there. Make sure they are well stocked with your brochures. See if they have any questions on your property. Help them be salespeople for you. They are there to help direct travelers to many things, including lodging.

If you are located in an area which is serviced by a Convention and Visitors' Bureau be certain to get involved. Their job is to sell your area to potential group business. Make sure they know you are willing to help with the effort. Your property may get first exposure to a potential group. Even if your property may be too small for the groups that the Bureau brings to the area, you will still be one of the first to hear of overflow potential.

Chapter 3 Identifying Your Target Markets

Become knowledgeable about all the types of business in your community. Do they have anyone who travels to visit them? How about the purveyors and sales people who call on them? Many times the people coming to visit these companies ask the company where they should stay. Make it your goal to get that recommendation. Sometimes they just ask the company to go ahead and make the reservation for them.

There is always a hierarchy with corporations. You may not think that some properties are suited for corporate travel. Possibly a motel is not suited for a CEO or one of the company's VIP's. It may be ideal for a young recruit of junior sales representative. Keep your mind and options as open as possible.

Don't overlook hidden potential that small companies may have. They may not be able to give you 100 room nights each year, but each one may have a handful of room nights to send your way. They also may have a personal reason for needing lodging in town. Wouldn't it be fantastic if they always stayed with you?

Your research in your community may show you that companies outside of the area are sending people into your area. Possible there is a new facility under construction or some other reason that they are coming. You will always want to consider where your room nights are originating and decide if you should focus some of your sales effort there.

> **Fortune favors the bold. — Juvenal**

You will also want to look to your competition for help in filling you property. Hopefully you had the opportunity while doing your competitive analysis to begin a relationship with the owners, managers or staff at these properties. Occasionally lodging properties in your area will book events that grow beyond their ability to accommodate all the guest rooms. This is especially true for hotels with meeting facilities. These group rates may be so low that the hotel will cut them off at a certain point, hoping to sell the remaining rooms at a higher rate. What this hotel considers a discounted rate may not be considered low for you. Establishing a good working relationship with key players at these properties can put you in the happy position of "helping" them out when they no longer can accommodate the group.

Look into the different event centers in your area that can be rented. If they do not offer guest rooms (which they probably do not), then you have found a possible revenue generator. Get to know the contact person at the facility. They are in a position to swing business your way as they try to help their clients plan events. Be sure they have brochures of your property on hand. Invite them over to tour your facilities. Take them to lunch. These people can be responsible for pushing a lot of business your way. How many of your competitors are showing this much desire to work with the event center? Remember, you are trying to out perform the competition. The event center also gives you the opportunity to offer meeting space to your potential groups, increasing *your* value.

Look to your local community as a source for business. Be involved with local sports clubs, political groups and social clubs. Cultivate influential residents in the community. Included would be the mayor and other high ranking city officials, but don't overlook players like the cab drivers. Sometimes they are the first representative a visitor will meet. Have them recommend your property.

Museums, theaters, galleries and other similar entertainment venues are quite often candidates for you guest rooms. These take some detective work to find potential business because individuals are probably responsible for their own travel arrangements.

Don't overlook freeway and highway traffic. This area can be an extension of all the market segments. There are many people who may just be tired of driving and need a room for the evening. A good example is truckers. If you have a fair amount of truckers passing your area consider contacting their main office to see if they may require accommodations.

Remember that because you will compete with different properties for different markets, you may find opportunity in unlikely areas. An example is a hotel in San Francisco had accepted a tour & travel series originating in Los Angeles. As the group drove up the California coast they were stopping for the night at roughly the half way point. At the time, a friend, Roxanne McDermott, was representing a property 45 minutes north of where they were staying the night. Roxanne contacted the group coordinator and the coordinator ended up moving the rest of the series to Roxanne's motel. The point being that possible business may currently be using a property 45 minutes away! Do not think too narrowly. There are many people who may be able to use your product and are not aware of it yet.

Locating Users for Your Property

This is a simple plan but highly effective in locating the most obvious users of your property. Find a map of your area and mark you location with a red X. Now mark all competitors with red dots. Take a ruler and find the mid measure – the half way mark – between you and each competitor. Connect these dots so that you enclose your property. Everything within this area is located in your "backyard". Speaking geographically, it is most convenient for the businesses inside this area to use your property than to use any others, your location is closest.

In the suburbs this area might cover a few miles, in a big city it may only be a couple blocks or a couple buildings. Regarding the geographical location, all the businesses located outside this area will find it more convenient to use one of your competitors. Work hard to capture all the business in your own backyard. Then venture out to attract other business.

Lessons From Your Competition

Now that you have looked at the other products you determined to be the competition, take another look at them but from a different perspective. This time, instead of looking at them through the eyes of a competitor, look at them

> **Put all your eggs in one basket and *watch that basket!*** — Mark Twain.

through the eyes of a potential user; a guest, tour operator, travel agent or company travel planner. Objectively examine the competition's product as a user and finish this sentence, "This is a nice hotel, but I would like to see..." Keep in mind just because another hotel or motel may be very unique it does not mean they are profitable or successful. With this new perspective you can consider if repositioning is right for you.

Repositioning

Thus far the projects have focused your attention on the realities of your property and those of your competitors. You have also given careful analysis to available markets and sources of business. Now you can focus on any changes that need to be made to your product before going after these new markets.

The goal of this book is to aid you in creating an effective marketing campaign. However, if your property is mediocre or is not yet suited for certain markets, your successful marketing and promotion can be the most expedient way to jeopardize your business. Word of mouth travels fast. Make certain you have it right for the first offering. You want the guests to return again and again.

By its nature, your small and efficient lodging property is probably better suited for marketing by **segmentation** as opposed to marketing by **differentiation**. But that is not to ignore differentiation, there is room for both in your marketing effort.

> Segmentation marketing: Identifying and addressing the needs of certain market segments.

Differentiation marketing: Highlighting the differences in your property compared to the other offerings in the marketplace.

Repositioning your property can give you the opportunity to combine these techniques. By identifying the segments your property will target you can address their specific needs and start a basis for differentiation.

You will want to focus your attention on what you can do best. Shave away all the nonessentials and concentrate on specific markets. You cannot be number one for all markets. Be absolutely clear with your direction.

➡Note the market segments that your property can realistically accommodate. Are there any necessary changes or alterations to make so you can better accommodate this business? For example, most tour companies require continental breakfast be made available to their guests. Others require they set up a direct bill account so your property will bill them for the rooms after the group checks out. Certain business from medical institutions in San Francisco ask that the hotel have video recorders available so the visiting doctors can go over their required tapes. Become a good detective. Ask lots of questions to uncover all the special needs. Some will not be worth pursuing, others can be quite profitable.

You may want to consider franchising your property or changing the existing franchise. This makes for a large part of repositioning as the franchise will dictate the upgrades needed. It may be expensive at the onset but a well selected and appropriate franchise can supply up to 30% of your room reservations. Today, franchises are as unique as snowflakes, and they seem to be that many to choose from. Contact the ones that fall in your market type and compare.

> You can't hold your head high with your hand out.
> — Yiddish Proverb

These changes, whether minute or drastic, are referred to as repositioning your property. Sometimes a property involved in repositioning will take on heavy capital expenditures, other times it is simply an overhaul of the amenities offered. Before you go any further, identify markets you want to target. Ask yourself what changes are necessary and how they will effect revenue. Finally, make certain you are *prepared* for the business from the market segments you are targeting before soliciting their business.

> Imagination is more important than knowledge.
> — Albert Einstein

Because markets are forever changing it is important to constantly and consistently look for ways to attract new business, and more importantly, keep the existing business. Often a property will loose revenue year after year – a steady downward spiral – because they do not want to change what *use to be* a very successful approach to filling their guest rooms.

Focusing on the guest is called *customer orientated marketing*. The opposite is called *product orientated marketing*. Keep your focus on the guest rather than your property and you will find new ways to increase your market share through the help of the guests' feedback.

Pricing

By focusing on *price*, your sales negotiating option will always be singular; to discount. Instead, focus on *value*. This gives you unlimited options. It is true that guests have become extremely price sensitive but it is only in relation to the value received.

Your pricing should have some logical basis. Many properties opened their doors and set room rates in accordance with that of their competition. This is sometimes known as the *market approach* to pricing because you set your rates at the same level as the rest of the market. Setting your rates this way doesn't give you the information you need in preparing special packages, discounting for groups and negotiating rates. A solid approach is to calculate from the bottom up. By backing into a rate structure, you can also take into consideration the return you require on your investment.

➲ Calculate your anticipated expenses for the year using your targeted occupancy and rate figures. Onto this sum add any rent or mortgage, interest, the minimum return on the capital you invested (probably your down payment), and any depreciation. With this figure you can see the total room revenue *needed*. From this point you can perform different if/then scenarios with targeted occupancies to see what average daily rate would be necessary in order to succeed.

In addition to this number crunching you will want to consider the different market segments you are targeting and the different types of business they will be bringing. The number of guest rooms and rate will be different with each source. Looking at it this way it may become apparent in order to achieve your net profit figure you will need to vary the market segment mix through a change in sales emphasis.

Chapter 4 Promotion

An Ongoing Effort

Promotion, advertising and marketing are ongoing efforts originating with the owner or management. The total effort should not be viewed as something to do when business is poor and needs a good kick in the rear. It should be a well thought out part of your long term marketing strategy. Any promotional effort will want to concentrate on three things:

- Getting the information across to the guest or potential guest,
- Reinforcing the desired behavior (having them use your property), and
- Engaging the curiosity of the first time guest to entice them to use your property.

A Look at Your Printed Material

Before you will attempt any promotional effort you will want to go over your printed material and make certain it is up to a level you can accept. Quite often the printed material is the only exposure a person can have with your property before making a reservation. It should be an honest and flattering representative. Our focus will be on your:

- Logo,
- Business cards,
- Brochures,
- Envelopes and invoices,
- Circulars and newsletters,
- Yellow page advertising,
- Billboards,
- Collateral inserts,
- Press releases,
- Fact sheet,
- Reprints, and
- Print advertising.

Logo. Develop a clean logo. This is critical. If you are not part of a franchise then you will have to come up with one on your own. Give it careful consideration. It is your identity. Before you have anything printed you will need to decide on your logo. It should be part of all your printed material.

Spend the money to have a professional create the logo for you. Once it is created you can always use a more economical printer who can adapt the camera ready artwork the top notch printer created. Spend the money up front and you are able to save it down the line. The creation of your logo is a one time expense. If you absolutely cannot afford this expense consider contacting your local university. The graphic arts students may welcome the opportunity to work on your design at a fraction of the cost.

Business cards. Use your business card like a mini brochure. Do not clutter it with every amenity you offer, but include the information that will help people make reservations. You can also mention those items which differentiate your property from your competition.

Brochures. Develop a clear and concise brochure to mail to prospective guests. Brochures can be mailed with the reservation confirmation letters. This gives people a visual aid while they are telling their friends where they will be staying. It will help to reinforce your name in people's minds.

Consider mailing a brochure with everything you send out, especially when sending correspondence or paying bills locally. You may want to include a small note asking it be passed on to the travel department. Never forget to include one with the travel agents' commission checks. You have already paid for the postage, use it to market your property.

When you are creating your brochures, have the photographs free of people. Hairstyles, clothes and makeup will quickly become outdated and your clientele may not be able to associate with the models. Still life gives your brochures longevity. Also, do not refer to your rates in your brochure. This will prove costly when your rates change. Instead, insert a rate card printed on a single-sheet, brochure size insert.

Envelopes and invoices. Do not miss advertising opportunities. Use all available printed material to promote your property. The outside of envelopes and billing statements are areas often overlooked by mediocre operators. You may want to create a concise slogan that differentiates your property to the potential guests. Incorporate it into your envelopes and invoices.

> An idea that is not dangerous is unworthy of being called an idea at all — Don Marquis.

One hotel company created envelopes especially for the travel agent commission checks that highlighted the benefits of their properties on the back side of the envelope. This is highly effective because it is a piece of mail that is certain to get opened and read.

Circulars and newsletters. Create circulars, newsletters or other mailing promotions. A simple way to work this is to work on a quarterly schedule. Every three months you should be able to create a one page newsletter which can be folded into thirds, addressed with a label and sent out. You can include special rate offerings, news in your area to entice business, renovation work, or to introduce a new desk clerk (also a great employee moral booster). This is an opportunity to brag about your property.

You can make people loyal to your property, but you have to be in consistent contact. Note it is not constant contact, but consistent. Your qualified contacts should hear from you every three to six months. Send these newsletters or circulars to keep contact with your qualified mailing list.

Yellow page advertising. Yellow page advertising may work if you expect a good portion of your business to be generated locally. Remember the possibility that the guest may originate from across the country but the reservation was made by someone locally. Also some properties find it effective to advertise in the yellow pages of the cities and counties that provide them with the most business.

Billboards. They can be a great resource if you get some walk-in business from the highway, freeway or interstate. Also if some of your reservations originate locally, a billboard can keep you in peoples' mind. This is reinforcement through repetition.

There is an extremely low cost in using a billboard relative to the number of people who are exposed to your message. The downside is that a billboard is not selective in the market segments it targets; many of the people exposed have no use for your offering.

Collateral inserts. Create single-sheet, brochure size inserts to inform people of special packages being offered. These can be inserted in the brochure to promote business at certain times during the year and then removed after the promotion is over. They are usually printed on lower cost paper stock than the brochure.

This affords you some flexibility and keeps printing costs low. Your rate cards should always be printed separately, never on the brochure. You may have to change your rates. To "doctor" a brochure looks unprofessional and to recreate is expensive.

Press releases. Also known as **news releases** because they include not only the print media but also releases to radio, television, certain sites on the World

Wide Web and other non-printed media. This is a highly effective form of free advertising. You will want to send press releases to the travel desk of newspapers in **feeder cities** to generate interest in your property and area.

> Feeder cities: Cities that provide travelers into your area, usually within two hours flight time. In a metropolis, the feeder cities consist of the cities serviced by shuttle flights.

Because this is a free form of advertising, you are able to use it for repetitive reinforcement to create name recognition. You can use the press release to announce any new changes to your property. Highlighting any recent renovation work, a new front office or sales manager, or special holiday room packages is always appropriate. News agencies appreciate the help. Often they are looking for filler information for the travel section of the paper. Also, send to your local media. Because of your location, you are automatically considered local news.

> Familiarity breeds contempt — Publilius Syrus.

Do not overlook trade publications. They are well suited for many of your press releases. Even though they do not speak directly to your potential guests, the information can create word of mouth advertising within the industry and many are targeted to travel agents. When creating your press releases, follow some simple guidelines:

- ♦ Always keep them one page in length and use a consistent layout,

Chapter 4
Promotion

- At the top of the page you will state "when", which should always be "For Immediate Release",
- Tap your creative juices and give the release a one line heading. This makes it easier for the editor, as they will not have to come up with the heading if yours is good,
- Use the same concise sentence structure you find in the publications you are addressing. Answer the questions who, what, where, why and when,
- Note who they should contact for additional information or for verification, and
- Three asterisks (* * *) or -30- at the bottom of the page signify the end of the press release.

Fact Sheet. Create a one page sheet listing the features of your property in very black and white terms. Spell out the number of rooms, room configurations (i.e. number of kings, queens and double bedded rooms), meeting space dimensions, and amenities offered. Many times a travel agent or a tour operator will ask you to fax over a fact sheet so they can see if your property can meet their requirements or so they may speak intelligently to a third party who may actually be making the reservations. Having this on hand can also save you much time and effort for individuals who call with basic questions regarding your property. By having a fact sheet handy you will have the option of faxing or mailing one to them if you feel it can answer their questions.

Reprints. Develop reprints of newsworthy items about your property to hand out, enclose in mailings or frame. If you are favorably written up in the local paper, travel section of another paper, or a travel or trade magazine, call the publication and ask them to send you a glossy reprint. Most are happy to oblige.

Have extras of these printed so you can include them in any sales kit you may give out. You can also have them framed and displayed around your front desk area. These will reinforce the idea that your guests have made the right decision by choosing your property.

Don't overlook any concise positive statements in the articles you can use elsewhere. If an article says your little motel is "...affordable and has the best views in all of Seattle," try to incorporate that quote in other printed promotional material. Help spread the word when people have nice things to say about your property.

Print advertising. Print advertising — taking out ads in magazines and newspapers — is definitely not for every property. In fact, only a few can really benefit from the expense. There are many forms of effective, affordable advertising and publicity, some of it free, and I suggest you pursue these first. If you decide you would like to pursue print advertising look first at trade publications. Studies have indicated for any type of business, the most cost effective form of advertising is in a trade publication. Trade publications speak to a selective group of individuals with a common interest. Because you have identified the markets you will target you should have an idea of their interests and the types of publications they read. Keep in mind women rarely subscribe to Popular Mechanics, children shy away from the Wall Street Journal, and young girls are unlikely candidates for a subscription to Men's Health. Understand the realities of your markets and you can then select the avenues that will be seen and heard by those markets.

Lodging properties in airport or destination cities can effectively advertise in in-flight magazines. Those are the complimentary copies located in the seat pocket on the airplane. It is easy to estimate in most situations fifty percent of the people on the flight are returning home. The other fifty percent, however, need a place to stay if they are staying the night. By featuring your property in an in-flight magazine (also a good place to send your press releases) you can focus your effort on the people who actually have a need for lodging in your area. A good place to start would be the in-flight magazines on the shuttle carriers from your feeder cities.

Remember when you deal in paid advertising you are dealing with sales people. They are selling the advertising to stay in business and their primary concern isn't for your lodging property. They want to see if they can be part of your marketing budget. Proceed with caution.

Advertising and Promoting On-Property

You can use the television in the guest rooms as a medium for advertising. With the purchase of a central video recorder and some wiring into the rooms, a dedicated channel can serve for in-house or community information. With some additional expense the in-room television can be programmed to default to that channel each time the television is turned on. This channel can grab a guest's attention and promotes your services, special packages and amenities.

Also consider marketing to your current guests so they stay for one extra night. (Just calculate what would happen if every reservation stayed one extra night!) You may want to create a small card you can place in their room the first night offering a discount if they extend their stay. This can be useful for weekend check-ins to get them to stay over Sunday night when your occupancy may be low.

Specialty Advertising

Advertising specialty gifts like pens, computer screen frames or key chains with your property's name and logo on them are nice to have to pass out when you are meeting with people that have the ability to book your property, such as during your sales calls. The downside of this form of advertising is that it is impossible to evaluate it's effectiveness. However, there are distinct situations where it helps you begin and maintain a relationship with someone that has the ability to fill your guest rooms. Most lodging property sales representatives wont go into a sales call without *something* to give to the travel agent or tour operator.

The item must have *some* value to the recipient. The idea is that they are getting something for nothing. Getting something for nothing is attractive for most people and the psychology behind this is the token gift creates a positive image in the mind of the recipient.

CHAPTER 4 73
PROMOTION

There may be something entirely unique about your property or location that will give you a good idea what to use. There is a hotel in San Francisco that gives out a yellow rubber ducky for the bathtub with their logo printed on the chest. The hotel itself is whimsical and the rubber ducky carries out the theme. Guests and clients love them. It reinforces the fun mood.

Practically any trade show you attend will have a booth for a company that caters to specialty advertising. Because every trade and industry has sales professionals, you will find the specialty advertisers at these shows. From the International Hotel/Motel & Restaurant Show in New York City to a software trade show in northern California, they will be represented. Sales and marketing is an integral part of any business. Get your hands on one of their catalogues. You will see you can have your logo printed on almost anything. If you decide not to take on the expense of this form of advertising at least have a firm idea of some affordable give away item that you can use during the holidays or on sales calls that can be related to your property. Some hotels in San Francisco pass out Ghiradelli chocolate squares to travel agents. They are affordable and very reminiscent of San Francisco, the home of the chocolate company.

Packages

Packages give you the opportunity to increase the perceived value your guests receive in exchange for the rates they pay. Many extras you can offer at little or no cost can mean a lot to certain people. Packages also allow you to continually offer something new to the guests you stay in contact with. Sometimes when you put everything in a package under one rate you aren't increasing your rate at all, the actual rate for the room after you subtract out the cost of the added amenities may be only a dollar or two above your average rate. However, the promotion may generate new guests and increase occupancy, not to mention the extras the guests may purchase from you in the way of telephone calls, food and beverage, or sundries. With increased occupancies comes the opportunity for increased *repeat* guests.

Using your package promotions in conjunction with your direct mail and press releases will create some talk about your property, and you will begin to whittle away at your competition. Packages can do three things:

- Push awareness with your potential guests,
- Help to keep employees excited about the property, and
- Constantly force you to think of new ideas to make your property more attractive to guests.

A package can be anything you can conjure up that is included in one rate. Often properties will include such items as a bottle of wine at check-in, an upgrade to the best available room, late check-out, tickets to a popular play or complimentary cocktails each evening. You may offer a rooms-only type package where after staying for three nights the guest gets the fourth night free, effectively increasing your average length of stay. A package that includes free parking is always enticing in

Chapter 4
Promotion

the big cities where the cost to park your car can be around $20 a day.

An idea that also reduces your cost is to tie in with other businesses. A local spa, the adjacent meeting facility without guest rooms, a recreational area and amusement parks are all dependent on guests and would welcome the people who stay at your property. Contact them to see if you can tie your sales effort together and get involved in a joint package/promotion.

You can create a family package with the nearby amusement park by including four day passes with the room rate and charging an amount lower than the family would pay if they purchased the tickets separately and paid your *rack* rate. The amusement park may even sell you the tickets at a discount in exchange for your marketing effort. You may also get the added benefit of the amusement park referring business to you because of the relationship you have.

Other packages can be created with this piggy back sales effort. Contact local restaurants. They may be interested in letting you create an envelope of dining coupons to give at check-in. This is of no extra cost to you, it benefits the guest as they are able to save money during the trip. An additional benefit is you are building a strong relationship with the local restaurants by referring business to them.

Co-op marketing can also help to mitigate the cost of promoting the package. Assume that you have created a two day stay package with a full body massage at a nearby health spa. In the print ad you will be effectively advertising your property, the health spa and the general package. The health spa should be ready to share the expense of the promotional advertising.

See if you can get your vendors involved in any promotions. If you have a beverage outlet on property contact the wine purveyor and invite them to host an evening wine reception for your guests and allow them to promote their product at the same time.

The planning that goes into these packages should involve a cost breakdown so you are certain to price it properly. There is nothing impressive about a guest figuring out he could have saved money by booking your room and buying his theater tickets separately. A solid and well thought out package cannot fail because of too much planning. A great many of them will because of too little.

Be creative and enthusiastic about your promotions. The entire planning process isn't all numbers and budgeting. It should be alive and fun. If you're not excited then your package is probably boring.

Direct Mail

In today's business climate it is becoming increasingly important to have your advertising dollars accountable. Many forms of advertising use a blanket approach where your message is put in front of many people but only a few of them are actually qualified buyers, or users, for your product. By creating a database you are able to control to whom you send your message.

CHAPTER 4 77
PROMOTION

With direct mail you can take the dollars you would spend on a newsprint ad, spend a *smaller* amount on a direct mail campaign focusing specifically on a target market, senior citizens for instance, and have money left over. The effort will be more focused and will most likely attract more guests than the newsprint ad, at a fraction of the expense.

From your direct mail campaign is something that industry people have termed the *echo effect*. This is the word of mouth of someone who received the mailing, the person who sees the mailing on the floor and picks it up, or anyone to whom the mailing wasn't sent. Some direct marketers say the bottom line results of a continual direct mail campaign that come from the echo effect are far greater than the response from the intended recipient. Of course this is all very difficult to measure, however guests who weren't on the direct mail list often request those promotional packages.

There are some people who believe there is little or no value in direct mail and it is not suited for the promotion of lodging properties. They consider it to be junk mail. However, research and my experience show that these ideas are not true. Managed correctly, your direct mail advertising can be a great source of guest reservations.

In comparison to other forms of advertising there are advantages to using direct mail. First of which is it is extremely selective. You have control over exactly who receives the offering. In this way you are able to target specific markets with specific promotions. You can concentrate on appropriate prospects rather than spending money on other forms of advertising, which usually sends a statement out to consumers at large.

Second is that you are connecting with people as close to a one on one basis as possible with out doing the actual sales call. Direct mail affords you personableness. Finally, if you prepare the promotion with forethought, it can be easy to calculate it's effectiveness.

But first to put things in perspective. An effective direct mail campaign will yield a 1% to 2% response. Anything more than that is outstanding, although it isn't uncommon for some finely tuned mailing lists created in-house to yield much more.

At the center of your mail effort is the database. A database is a repository of addressing and contact information, from both existing and prospective guests, as well as those responsible for making reservations. The database will enable you to target the specific markets that you outlined in chapter two. You can also tailor mailings to each one of the markets you have chosen.

The list you use is the most important part of your effort. You can send the most outstanding offering to people who have absolutely no use for it and the results will be next to nothing. Conversely, you can mail a slop-job mailing of a lodging package to a qualified list of people who can use it and the response can be very high. You can either rent a list from a company that deals with the same clientele that would use your product or you can create one in-house.

The highest quality list is the one that you create and manage yourself. This is called your *in-house* list. Most likely this is a list of guests who have already stayed with you or have contacted you for information on your property. The people on this list have already qualified themselves as users and potential users of your product. They are already familiar with your property and they are comfortable with your property and services. These people should be contacted consistently.

The creation of your list is an ongoing process. The best place to start is your own registration records. These records already give you a wealth of information. In addition to the basic name and mailing address, you will also find information on who made the reservation. Sometimes you will find that the traveler is from Santa Fe but the reservation originated out of a travel agency in Albuquerque. If this agency is responsible for travel that comes into your area then they should be included in your database. Other information found could be length of stay patterns (good to know when creating packages to promote longer stays), method of payment, business or leisure travel, and whether they are repeat guests.

There is a certain problem in using registration records as a database for mailing lists because eventually the size will be too great and you will only want to mail to those with the ability to return as guests another time. Some may argue to only use those names that are repeat guests, the point being they have been there twice and have already proved they do come back into your area. However, these people are already using your property. The idea is to maintain this guest base with quality service and invite people who have stayed with other properties in the past to sample what you have to offer.

A way to work through this is to question guests at the front desk and use your judgment call as to whether you want to include them in your database. You can also leave a book in the lobby area where you can invite them to fill out if they would want to be on your mailing list. Any names and address of people you consider to have repeat potential should be included.

Along with your valued guests, you will want to cultivate heavy hitters and keep them on your mailing lists. Heavy hitters are those people who have the ability to give you many room nights each year. There is a travel agency in El Segundo, California that booked around 2,500 room nights a year into the town of Sunnyvale, California for individuals traveling to firms specializing in engineering for defense. In this agency there are three agents who actually booked these rooms. These three agents were heavy hitters. Any property in Sunnyvale should have been in contact with this agency, even if their motel or hotel didn't necessarily meet the criteria requested by the agents. There were times when the city of Sunnyvale was impacted and guest rooms were hard to come by. The agents had to look for alternative properties. Chapter five will cover locating leads for potential business in more detail. The qualified ones should be part of your database.

With your in-house list you will consistently want to maintain it. Twenty percent of the American population moves every year. This is over fifty million people. A five year old mailing list is entirely obsolete. Be sure to update address changes as you find out about them and check for duplicate entries. Sometimes you can end up with the same individual at two addresses, their former and present address. Use the phone to conduct teleresearch on the contacts in your database. By speaking directly with the consumers once in a while you can secure information that may be able to directly impact reservations and keep your database information clean and accurate. The building of a great in-house list does not stop after you enter the names into the computer. This information allows you to begin building a relationship with your guests and users.

Creating a list yourself can be a slow process, although the quality can be much higher than something that you rent. Experts have said an in-house list should generate anywhere from two to ten times the response of a rented list. Most associations and organizations will rent their lists to you. These may be a place to start if you currently have a short or weak list. You can look at the *Encyclopedia of Associations* or other references in the library to find one that will fit your offering. After you rent a list, you are entitled to solicit, and include in your in-house list, the people from the rented list that responded to your offering.

There are some basic rules to direct marketing and you will want to follow them very close. This is not an area for you to be innovative. Because the return (1%) is low, you will not want to make any mistakes. There are many books out there you can check from the local library on the subject of direct mail. I encourage you to read a few and get a good handle on the objectives you want to achieve and how you can realistically go about doing them. A good program to follow is to do what has been proven to work and use your creativity on the contents of the promotion.

There are tried and true formulas for direct mail. The main component being consistency. In addition to the one percent response rate you will also be planting seeds for future reservations. Some recipients will not have a need at the time of your mailing. When you are consistent in letting them know you value their business, they will think of you when the time comes for them to make the reservation.

Focus on the envelope used in the mailing, or the outside of the tri-fold if that is how your mailing will be sent. This area *must* capture the attention of the recipient. Today, people are savvy to unsolicited mail. Just by looking around the post office you will see many people throwing out a large amount of mail unopened. It doesn't matter how impressive your offering is if they don't open the envelope. All your creative effort is for naught if they never see the inside. Make the envelope perform its function; to entice the recipient to open it.

People in the advertising industry call the printed information on the outside, apart from the addressing and return addressing, the *teaser copy*. This is the slogan, sentence, or imperative you print on the outside to lure the reader to open the envelope to learn more! Remember after the envelope is opened it most often will go straight into the waste basket. It is reassuring to the reader to see the tag line or teaser copy is printed again on the inside of the mailing. This way you're certain the impressive slogan you created will not be forgotten.

Your mailing must grab their attention to ensure it gets read and remembered. Ultimately you want the recipient to act immediately to your offering. This action is your goal. This may sound rudimentary but it is vital; always include a phone number for them to use. If it is in your budget, make it a toll free number. Often people will be mildly interested and are only inquiring.

Chapter 4
Promotion

These people will probably only inquire if the call costs them nothing.

With these inquiries, you have the opportunity to speak with them and close a sale. There is still gold to be found even if they let you know they are not ready to make a reservation, but are just shopping. You now have a live person to speak with, to find out what they are looking for in a lodging facility, and see if you can meet their needs. You may be able to close some of these sales as well, or get a phone number so you can call them in a week to see if you can offer any more assistance with their travel plans.

The purpose of your mailing is to get your reservation's line to ring. Be concise and give just enough information so they will act or call for more information. Make it exciting. The copy should let them know it is something they desire. Use the bullet format as opposed to paragraphs. Bullets are much easier for people to read and retain the information. Quite often people will not read everything, but will skim over the mailing to get the general idea. Have your mailing work double duty by combining an awareness building campaign into the direct response, which is to make a reservation now. Make it simple to understand what it is you want them to do. At the bottom write, "Call today to book XYZ package, 800-555-1234."

Have them ask for a specific offering, like the *Summer Sizzle Package*. This gives you a way to track the effectiveness of your mailing because you will know exactly what prompted that person to make the reservation. Over time you can compare what packages did well for which markets. Incidentally, when you are taking a reservation it is a good idea to ask them how they came to decide on your establishment. This one question will give you a wealth of information.

Other uses for your database can be for holiday cards and thank-you-for-your-business notes. You might even consider using your property's post card in place of the actual thank you card. This way they will have a clear picture of your property in their mind for reference. Just make certain it is a flattering photograph. The impact of thank you notes can be monumental.

Because you are creating a Sales and Marketing Plan for a full year out, you have the ability to create your future mailings well in advance of the promotions mentioned. This affords you the opportunity to take advantage of lower class postage and their lower rates. Just be certain you give them adequate time to arrive. You don't want your holiday cards arriving in mid-January.

The purpose of your direct mail campaign is simple and singular; to get them to call or stop by your property. Once that is done the mailing piece has done it's job. The piece is not expected to make them book the room. Now that you have them on the phone or in front of you at the desk, it is *your* job to see the reservation is made.

E-mail, the World Wide Web and the Internet

When fax machines arrived, it wasn't long before their widespread acceptance as a valuable tool for conducting day to day business. Try to imagine conducting your operation without one. Most everyone has their fax number printed on their business cards and all other stationary. With the trends as they are, the same should hold true for your e-mail address, and eventually your web site address.

Internet advertising can be a very cost effective approach to attract an educated market base with a higher average income. The marketing of lodging properties and travel destinations is growing fast on the World Wide Web (WWW). Research companies have showed that second only to the sale of computer products, the most active marketing on the Internet is that of travel.

This section is only meant as an informative overview of using on-line services, web sites, the Internet and e-mail to add to your property marketing. This information changes rapidly and you will want to consult experts in this field should you decide to create a web site or participate in one that caters to marketing your type of property. If you have never been on-line you should get your feet wet before making the financial commitment to marketing through a web site. The major services such as America Online, CompuServe and Prodigy now offer promotions where up to your first 50 hours are free. You can locate their software easily. It usually can be found inserted in computer related magazines, or you can simply call and they will send it out right away. If you don't have a computer you will probably want to get one for reasons other than the Internet at some point. When that time comes, there will most likely be Internet software pre-installed on the system that you can try out.

On-line services are not the Internet. They are self contained cyber-communities that you belong to with a large group of other people. They all now have some sort of Internet access. If you belong to America Online you cannot visit forums in CompuServe. You are limited to the forums of America Online or the vast reaches of the Internet. Conversely, if you are a CompuServe subscriber you cannot visit the forums of America Online but only those of CompuServe, or once again, the Internet.

You can access the Internet and the WWW without using an on-line service, but many people find on-line services easy to navigate and more user-friendly. If you opt to go without the on-line service you will need to get Internet browser software like Microsoft Internet Explorer or Netscape Navigator. In addition to this you will need an Internet Service Provider (ISP). This is the computer that your computer will call up to access the Internet. At press time, this service is running about $19.95 per month for unlimited access.

However you access, either through an on-line service or an ISP, you will have access to e-mail. E-mail is the tool most widely used through these services. You are able to e-mail from your address at any service to another at any service. That is to say that you can subscribe to America Online and e-mail a friend or client at CompuServe or one who's address is hosted by an ISP. E-mail is not platform sensitive – it doesn't matter whether you use a Macintosh operating system, a Windows environment or any other – you can send and receive mail. E-mail is an effective way to send messages quickly and inexpensively. If you have your clients e-mail address you can send them an electronic newsletter of your hotel or motel very quickly with little cost. Remember to respond to e-mail quickly. Internet users have a need for instant gratification. The faster you respond, the better. Be sure to check your e-mail daily. You don't want to respond to an availability request for December the 14th after the date has passed.

One attractive aspect of marketing on the WWW is it levels the playing field. A small inn and a large hotel can have the same presence on a screen. It is not easy for the viewer to know if you are a mom and pop operation or a large organization. Everyone can create an attractive, informative and entertaining web site.

The thing to remember about the Internet is that people use it primarily for information and secondly for entertainment. Your site will want to address these two points in some way. You will also want to start small and see where your successes will be. Don't let someone talk you into spending a lot of money at the onset. After the creation of a site and registering a **domain name** you can find a company to host your site for as little as $100 per year.

> Domain name: To interpret the hotel company's address www.holiday_inn.com, the *www* stands for the World Wide Web and *holiday_inn.com* is the domain name. The entire configuration is the address. Internet users will key in this specific address into a browser such as Microsoft Internet Explorer or Netscape to download your page. An organization called InterNIC in Virginia manages the distribution of domain names and records them. There is a charge of $50 per year. No two domain names are alike.

If you have decided you want to pursue a site on the World Wide Web, you have three options in constructing it; doing it yourself with software such as Microsoft's FrontPage, Corel WEB.DESIGNER, HotMetaL PRO, you can have an advertising agency design it (very expensive), or you can use a firm that specializes in web site creation.

Creating an interesting and informative web site alone will add nothing to your reservation base. Your web site will need to be locatable. The first step in getting reservations and increased booking from the Internet is to get people to visit your web site. There are three parts to this. First, you will want to have your web site address located on all your printed collateral, your advertisements, yellow page advertisements, match books, et al. You have to *promote* your web site, educate people that your site exists and mix it in with your print media and collateral. That is why you will see www.companyname.com on television, billboard and all other advertising. They want you to be aware of their web address so that you can easily find them. This is a convenience for the people who already know your company exists and makes it easy for the techno-savvy to get information about your property and to make the reservation.

The second part is to make your site easy to call up if the person does not have your web address and has to use a search engine. A search engine is a program you access via the search engine's web site on the Internet and enter some clues as to what you are looking for. The search engine will search the entire Internet for comparables and matches to the data, retrieve those addresses and list them for the user to browse. The user then can choose which to visit. Many of these search engines check the frequency of words on web sites and give more importance to frequent words. For example if you are a hotel in Napa it seems logical that anyone looking for a hotel in Napa would enter at least those two words; **hotel napa**. The search engine will bring back the addresses of those sites where those words are located and list them in the order of the most frequent mentions. It would be to that hotels benefit to have those words appear often in the verbiage. However, you will not want to overdo it. Some search engines throw out words that are mentioned over six times. Consult some of the major services for search engines at their web sites. These are the more popular ones:

- Yahoo!: www.yahoo.com
- Lycos: www.lycos.com
- Infoseek: www.infoseek.com
- AltaVista: www.altavista.com

Third, team up with others in your geographical area who have web sites and place *hot links* on each others' site to increase the number of hits each site will get. A hot link is a place on the web site where the user can click on with the mouse to be transported to another web site without having to fill in the address of the new web site. It makes sense that if you are a hotel in Napa you will want to be locatable through other Napa attraction web sites. If someone is planning a trip to Napa and are looking at the sites of attractions it makes sense they may need accommodations. The host web site may charge you to place a hot link on their page as they have probably spent money to promote it and your hot link offers the visitor a chance to get away. Sometimes you can agree on having a reciprocal link on your page to get to their site. Hot links increase traffic to your site as you can reap the rewards of another company's web site marketing efforts.

Certain information is a must on your web site other than your property description and reservation number. You will want to include something on the site that is a *call to action.* You will have extended much promotional effort to get someone to visit your web site so don't let them leave without giving you some way to contact them in the future. You may offer a chance to win a weekend getaway or a special package. The idea is to get them to fill out a on-line form that they will enter their name, address, e-mail address and other information you can use. You can add these pre-qualified people to your database. Also because you get their e-mail address, you can send them a message to visit your web site when you update it or add some special package, all at the click of your mouse.

Getting in the Guide Books

Many travelers make all their lodging choices from listings in guide books. The AAA books are probably the most well known and the most used. In turn they are also one of the most expensive. To be listed in the AAA guide book a AAA representative must visit your property to see if it is in accordance with the standards they have set. If you do meet their minimum requirements then you will be given a rating between one and four diamonds. To begin the process, contact your local AAA office.

There are many other books that you can be listed in and many are free of charge. If they are free of charge then there is little reason not to pursue them. These books change frequently so you will want to get in the ones that are currently *en vogue*. This will require a trip to your local bookstore. A library is a good second choice but the bookstore will have the most recent copies. Take a pen and notepad with you and write down the contact information for those that would work for your particular property.

Once contacted, many of the guide books will fax over a form to fill out regarding your property description. It may be wise to offer a special package or rate for the readers of that particular book. This way the caller will tell you how they heard about you and you can track the effectiveness. Many times the listing is free of charge because they need to create a comprehensive and thick book. However, the publication will most likely offer you the opportunity to upgrade your listing with color photographs and detailed descriptions for a fee. As with all forms of advertising, consider the cost against the anticipated return and make an informed decision.

Contact Lanier Publishing International, LTD. P.O. Box D, Petaluma, CA 94953, (707) 763-0271; Fax (707) 763-5762. They publish a series of directories for accommodations including bed and breakfasts, inns, small hotels, resorts, condos and all-suite hotels. Their titles are also published electronically on CompuServe, America Online and the Microsoft Network.

Also investigate the other guide books on the World Wide Web. The typical user of the Internet has a considerable larger disposable income than the average American and enjoys traveling. Once again, if the listing is free there is little reason not to participate. If it is available for a fee, consider it and your other advertising options.

Promotional Strategy

There are many avenues to consider in promoting your property. You will want to consider carefully the markets for which you will compete and the best approach for your property in regards to all the material covered in this chapter. Your promotional strategy outlines the printed material you will create, the specialty advertising items you will use to promote your hotel or motel, the packages to entice reservations, your direct mail frequency and its contents and any advertising, web sites, e-mail or Internet marketing.

➡On a sheet of paper, list everything in full detail regarding your promotional strategy. Include the dates you plan to initiate each promotional point, and all the tasks necessary to accomplish the promotional point. If it is printed material or something else that you will be ordering, state the quantity and the date you will order, as well as the date in which you plan to create and approve the drafts. Save this sheet as you will need it in Chapter 8. You can allow yourself to be loose in your commitment to this promotional strategy. As you continue to read this book you may find that you will want to change some ideas. The point is to get you thinking about it now and to get your ideas down on paper. You can fine tune it in Chapter 8 as you integrate it into the action plan.

Chapter 5 Sales and Selling

Marketing Compared to Selling

The key to successfully filling your guest rooms, increasing your occupancy, your rate, your revPAR, and achieving the profitable mix of market segments you set for your property is to put the marketing first and the selling second. The marketing is everything you do to generate interest and develop inquiries. Selling is taking the leads the marketing has generated and turning them into room bookings. The Marketing Plan is often called the Sales and Marketing Plan because it outlines the objectives, strategies and tactics for both the marketing and the selling of your guest rooms and amenities. The marketing has to come first.

> **There is nothing more demoralizing than a small but adequate income. — Edmund Wilson**

Everything thus far has focused on identifying the market segments that are most suited to book and use your hotel or motel. Your sales effort can never succeed if you have not intelligently interpreted the data in targeting appropriate markets.

To effectively market and sell your property, you must have an understanding of four things. You have to be well versed in all four because they operate as a team to fill guest rooms. If one is missing, the others are not effective. These important four items to know and understand are:

- Your product offered (your property),
- The clients (who will use your property),
- The art of selling, and
- How to speak of the benefits of your product to the client.

You have been focusing on learning about the product you offer, now we will look at the other three. Your sales effort is mapped out in your marketing plan. Before you will write your plan you will be introduced to the normal functions of the lodging sales professional. This chapter is by no means a comprehensive or complete guide to sales. Quite the contrary. There are endless books written on the subject of sales. You are urged to read them voraciously. Every type of business involves the sale of something. For the most part the skills for sales are transferable from one industry to the next, and can be used to fill your guest rooms. The attempt of this chapter is to show you the subtleties that are particular to lodging sales and how to apply sales to fill your guest rooms.

Chapter 5
Sales and Selling

All the sales activity you initiate should aim for three goals; one, to get you in front of the person who can make the decision, two, to get them in to see and tour your property and, three, to identify the available uses your property can have for them and act on them. Your marketing and telephone sales should focus on these objectives. Keep them in mind when writing promotional mail material, brochures and press releases. The end result of all these should be contact between you and potential users and/or guests.

Be cognizant of what you are selling. People make their purchase decision based on emotion. After they have made the decision to purchase they will need to support (read: justify) their decision with logic. You are not selling a 12 x 14 room for a night. Think about what you are offering; a good night's sleep, security, convenience, atmosphere, relaxation, and many others. Maybe they want to impress their friends with the claim they stayed with you. With these you can appeal to their emotions. After you have sold them emotionally you may have to assist them by providing logical reasons to support the decision.

Emotions Dictate Purchase Decisions

Recently I was on vacation and found I needed to purchase a pair of hiking boots. I was in the Footlocker in Waikiki and carefully looked over the selection till I decided on two I liked. One was $100 and the other $180. It was just my luck I was more attracted to the $180 Nike Air hiking boots and not the less expensive pair. Mentally I had decided that I would be much better off with the Nike Air, albeit aesthetically. With the emotional decision made, I read through all the available pamphlets enclosed in the boxes till I could justify the purchase; they were Goretex, they would last 100 years, I'd *never* have to buy another pair. With the $100 pair, I reasoned they would only last two years and my feet would invariably get wet. I justified the purchase *logically* after I had made it *emotionally*.

So what is it that you are selling? Always keep in mind that those infomercials at night aren't selling AbRollers and AbCrunchers. They are selling you a well defined, fat free, muscular, washboard stomach. That is what brings you to the phone with your credit card in hand. Cellular phone companies aren't selling phones, they're selling freedom, mobility, prestige and safety. In the same respect consider what it is you are selling.

Most likely, you and your competitors are all offering a bed, shelter and a bathroom. Sell the differentiation; a good night's sleep, escape from the pressures of the office, relaxation. Demonstrate how they can impress their significant other or customers by being able to say they stayed with you. Show them the contentment you offer. Give them a sample of the ambiance and atmosphere.

In order for someone to buy what it is you're selling they have to believe the value is there. Is the price paid in proportion to the perceived benefit? If it is, then there is perceived value in the eyes of the buyer.

CHAPTER 5
SALES AND SELLING

Word of Mouth

Because your product is a de facto service, your sales effort will rely heavily on your reputation. A good night's sleep is not something a potential tour operator can hold and examine for quality craftsmanship. The closest you can get to tangibility is to have them stay in or visit your property.

It is often said the best form of selling is word of mouth. Unfortunately your control over this medium is minimal. Your best strategy is to be diligent in maintaining the integrity of your offering to keep the word of mouth positive and possibly coaxing it along to speed up the process. People take good service for granted and not often will they go to great lengths to pass the word. Conversely, if the service or experience is lousy, they will frequently go out of their way to tell as many people as possible. Bad word of mouth is more damaging than good word of mouth is helpful.

Marketing your property through word of mouth is critical so make it effective. This alone can be responsible for a sizable chunk of your business. You will want to do everything to maintain a good reputation. Work on increasing the impact of good word of mouth. Make certain to ask your guests to tell others of their great experience. Sometimes people need a little nudge to share good information. Remind them to take along your brochure to pass along, or at least your name and phone number. If you have appreciation parties for businesses that book your property, it may be wise to invite community leader. The idea is to promote their good word of mouth.

Profile of the Professional Salesperson

Because you are running your marketing effort on a tight budget you will probably be the salesperson for your property. Even if you have the luxury of hiring a salesperson, you will want to have a working knowledge of what should be expected of them, as well as be able to pitch in and help if you should find yourself in a situation where you are able to bring some guest room reservations back from wherever you may be. If you are a franchise affiliate, then you will have a clearer picture what their sales staff should do for you.

Live the salesperson. That which differentiates the superstars from the other players in the world of sales is that **the superstars are those that are always aware of the selling potential of every situation.** A solid idea is to work it into every conversation that you own a lodging property and if that person should ever have a need for your type of facility, they should give you a call. Tell them you would appreciate and take care of any business they should send your way. Give them your personal line to make the reservation. You will be amazed at the amount of business that you will uncover this way. Everyone will know of someone, sometime, that can use a motel or hotel room. Hand out your business cards. They wont do any good unless you can get them into the hands of the people that can use them.

Have lifetime goals. This book is designed to help you establish goals and objectives in regards to your property. Goals are the thrust of successful sales people. They also apply the same goal techniques to all

Chapter 5
Sales and Selling

areas of their lives. To reach the top you must have direction. Set a plan to reach your dreams.

Continue your education. It has been said when you're green you grow and when you're ripe you rot. The great salespeople understand that they do not know and can never know it all in terms of selling. They continually take courses in sales and marketing and so should you. Look into the colleges in your area or check the business sections of the local paper. There may be classes, lectures or seminars coming to town that can rejuvenate your selling or give you the skills you need. A very inexpensive source is your local library. Take advantage of it and get books that will sharpen your sales skills. Also remember to review the basics of selling every so often. Many professionals recommend once a year to either read a book on the topic of sales or attend a sales or motivational seminar.

Be a teacher. It is important that when you are out speaking with people to be informative. **People listen to a teacher but rarely a salesperson.** Form your presentations and conversations so those listening can walk away with something learned. You don't necessarily have to have the teaching aspect be about your property, it can be on some attraction or development in your area. After you have their attention you can shift gears to talk about your property and how it can meet their needs. Make sure you are well versed with what is going on in your area and what it has to offer. Stay current with developments in your area. An intelligent way to do this is to consult research studies such as those found at the Chamber of Commerce and in trade magazines to get further insight on your business and community. A wealth of information can also come from reading the local paper.

The paper is also a good source for ideas of where to locate new business.

Subscribe to newspapers or magazines of the groups you intend to do business together. If you have decided to target the senior traveler market then you better subscribe to magazines that focus on issues that are important to them. This will not only give you command of relevant issues so you may talk intelligently with the guests but also it will point out concerns and needs you may be able to fill. Many times articles will list some of the relevant players in their market or industry. It may be wise to contact them or at least put them on your mailing list.

Join activities and organizations and become involved with your community. Because your business is hospitality, it only makes sense you should be social to attract new business. Get out of your office and get involved in community activities. Joining organizations, especially charitable ones, is a great way to interact with the people in your area, create good will for your property and give something back to your community. Other than charitable organizations there are business groups you can join. Choose activities and organizations that interest you. By enjoying what you do you can insure you will always remain active.

You can also join roundtables to sharpen your market savvy. Many of these discussion groups can be found at the Chamber of Commerce and often they focus on bringing businesses into the community. Offer to lead the telemarketing campaign or the letter writing campaign. Often you can use your property's letterhead as you write on behalf of the community. This is a good

Chapter 5
Sales and Selling

way to introduce your property to people who may be coming to visit the area soon.

It is wise to host some of the events at your property. This will give you some needed exposure. Hosting the monthly Chamber of Commerce mixer is a way to get business leaders to see and become aware of your property. Always have some guest rooms available to show to satisfy their curiosity. Remember you are hosting the event so don't skimp on the hors d'oeuvres and refreshments, you are trying to make a positive impression.

You may want to consider sponsoring events that are not on your property. You can either give money to the event or possibly supply some needed guest rooms for use during the event or in the future. They may be able to raffle off the room gift certificates to help raise money. Depending on the event, in exchange for your generous donation, they may place your name and/or logo in their promotional material, mention your sponsorship at the event, display your signage or any combination of the three.

Joining activities will help to develop good relations with the community. Beyond just liking and trusting you, if they know you personally you can better build their loyalty. Hopefully this will weigh in your property's favor when their Aunt Betty comes to town to visit or they are responsible for finding rooms for their sister's wedding. It can never hurt to be on a personal level with community leaders.

Track the local sporting events to locate opportunities to accommodate out of town guests. Many visiting team fans will not want to make the trip back the same day as the game. Consider advertising in their publications and offering special rates or late check-out. Your local paper is a good source of all the upcoming games. Contact them to see if they have a schedule for the year and who you could contact for each team.

Get to know the coaches of the local teams. Often the out-of-town coaches will contact them to get recommendations regarding where they should stay. Have it be your property.

Rehearse your presentation. You will want to focus the energy to build strong communication skills. Communication is the master tool of any sales professional, you will want to make sure that it is always well oiled. By rehearsing your presentation you will always get the important points across. It is not to say that you should have it memorized, line by line, verbatim. Practice in front of the mirror until it flows in a casual and conversational manner. If you are eloquent you will keep their interest longer.

Recruit and delegate. Once you get a good grasp of the subject, pass on some sales information to your entire staff. One hotelier said he considers his entire staff to be his sales department. This is glaringly obvious when you consider that departments like housekeeping have a high degree of guest contact. It is critical that the concepts of sales and marketing are understood and practiced by all your employees. Teach them the importance of guest orientation in all that they do. Guest satisfaction should be their priority. This concept will not be instilled in your employees by accident, you must make a dedicated effort.

> The sharp employ the sharp — Douglas Jerrold.

A related note to your entire staff as salespeople is that you should pay particular attention to the people who you hire that have first contact with guests. All too often owners and managers will hire without checking the references or the credentials of the applicant. If you put the right person with the right job at the onset, your sales and marketing training will have more impact. No matter what job you are hiring for, check for that potential employee's selling abilities. Pay attention to appearance, personality and the sales skills they already posses.

Cultivating Leads

Uncovering potential users of your property may seem daunting. Many people have a fear of approaching strangers or calling an unknown person and asking for their business. It may not sound comforting to the fledgling sales person but it does get easier as you do it. Much frustration can be had from focusing your sales effort on a market that has little or no need for guest rooms at your establishment. It can be less of a chore if you put your sales talents to work on qualified people or companies. You will want to generate leads for yourself to call on. As outlined below, there are many ways to locate potential clients. You may want to refer to chapter two; Sources of Business for additional ideas.

Past clients. It is true that it is easier and less expensive to keep the guests you already have than to go out and try to replace them with new business. Many properties often lose sight of a treasure trove of potential business; the past groups and guests of the lodging establishment. These are obvious users of your property because you have served them before and they have demonstrated a need for lodging in your area and your type of property. This can also be an ideal way to begin your database. Check past guest histories to find the ones where the guest gave the company name of a local business. These would be good people to call to see if there is a particular person in their company that handles the travel arrangements that you can contact. Attempt to get into their preferred hotel listing. Many companies prepare a list of properties in different cities with rates for their employees to use while on business travel. Contact the travel agencies that booked previous guests to see if they handle a lot of travel into your area.

Work your competition. Another fine reason to be intimate with your competition is to develop them as a source of business for you. Many times sales people cannot use the leads they have developed because of various reasons. These reasons can range from price to location to the desired dates being unavailable. Cultivate relationships with your competitors so you are the first person they think of if they cannot take a group. Do the same for them and you have a win-win situation.

Maximize contact time with guests. Talk and listen to the people who are currently staying with you. They can provide a world of information regarding what they like and dislike about your property, amenities they would like to see provided, obstacles that need addressing in your sales presentation or leads for potential business. **Get out of your office and visit with these people.** You can't create business for your hotel or motel by hiding behind closed doors. Sales is

Chapter 5
Sales and Selling

an interactive pursuit. Feel good about yourself every time you get out to meet the people who stay with you.

You may want to offer a complimentary evening wine cr tea reception in your lobby nightly as part of the amenities you extend. By having it nightly between 5:00 p.m. and 6:00 p.m. you can spend time visiting with the guests, getting valuable feedback from them and add to the *perceived value* of the rate paid.

Cultivate key clients and heavy hitters. These are the people who can fill your property, either directly or through referrals. Good sources are the travel agents that currently use your property, Convention and Visitors' Bureaus, nearby businesses and training schools. There are hundred of others you can probably think of. Look into your backyard for leads. Talk to all the shop owners in your area and invite them to recommend your property to the salespeople that call on them. Find out if they have any need for rooms themselves.

If you do a good job at cultivating the heavy hitters and getting to know the key people in your industry, you may be able to ask them to provide you with some good lists of contacts. By maintaining a strong relationship with these people you can keep your interests in the forefront of their thought. Possibly when they are looking through a trade publication they could come across a list of the Top Ten Travel Agencies in Tennessee, or the Fastest Growing Companies in your community. It would be to your benefit if they were to pass this on to you. Also these heavy hitters may have lists of their own they can share with you.

Good contacts are necessary for good referrals. Look to the people in your community who others go to for help and advice. Who's word is considered golden? A recommendation from a heavy hitter is worth its weight in gold. Get them to refer business to you and always express your thanks for any referral. Write a thank you note letting them know you appreciate them sending business your way and they can rest assured you will take good care of anyone they send. Your gratitude will land you more referrals.

Work to form a strong bond with these people. Take the hot prospects — the ones that can really impact room reservations — out to lunch once in a while. The key is to make them feel that they are obligated to send you business so be certain to pick up the tab. If they pay they may feel that they have fulfilled their obligation.

Don't forget the less obvious heavy hitters like taxi cab drivers, bartenders and others who are in a position to recommend your property. Get to know them and ask for their referrals.

Master telemarketing. Done properly, telemarketing is a cost effective way to uncover additional business for your hotel or motel. Many people fear cold calling on a business by dropping in at their location without an appointment. For most, it is much wiser to begin with prospecting by telemarketing. You can then set up appointments with the qualified leads you found. Many have a fear of getting on the phone and soliciting business from strangers. It doesn't have to be a painful experience and with a good list of people to call you will find business. There is a science to telemarketing, and like your direct mail campaign, the system is tried and

Chapter 5
Sales and Selling

true. It doesn't afford much variation. Stick with the basics and you will reap results.

There are many advantages to telemarketing over the in-person sales call. Aside from the fact that you don't necessarily have to *look* presentable, you can cover much more ground in terms of the number of people you contact. On a powerful day you may only see ten to fifteen people with in-person sales calls, however on the telephone you can easily call forty to fifty. Following are the basics for a well put together telemarketing campaign:

- Decide beforehand what it is you want to get across to the people you will call,
- Always have the name of the person you will be speaking with beforehand,
- Be certain you are in an area and time you can be free of interruptions,
- Have some sort of contact sheet in front of you (their file if you've called them before) to write notes and confirm addresses and phone numbers,
- Introduce yourself in the first sentence,
- Keep it short and to the point, and
- Follow up, follow up, follow up.

☛It is wise to prepare for the phone call in the same way you would prepare for an in person sales call. You must rehearse your presentation until you can deliver it in a confident and conversational manner. Start by identifying the purpose of your call. Are you calling to ask about the amount of travel they have coming into your area? Will you call to thank them for the business they have sent you and would like to know if there was something you could do to receive all of their travel into your town? Write down the reason of your call so it is clear to you. Now write beside it what it is that you want them to do or what information you want to get from them. This is your objective and your call is successful if you accomplish this before they hang up.

Now that you have your objective in mind, create a short script of what you will say in the ideal call. Write it down word for word and remember to keep it short and to the point. Practice saying it aloud. Listen to how it sounds. Keep the opening remark to; Hello, this is Joe Wolosz with the Bayside View Inn of San Francisco. Can I speak with Mr. Doyle? Always identify yourself clearly and with confidence. Once the desired person comes on the line, identify yourself and state the reason for your call. Memorize your script so you can say it with confidence and are able to modify it to the different directions a call can take.

Always have a list in front of you of who it is you will be calling and set aside a block of time to move through that list without interruption. Successful sales people clear everything that would be in the way of their selling time. This is wise for both telephone sales and your in person calls. When telephoning to uncover leads, you shouldn't even let the phone hit the cradle till you have completed all the calls. Keep the hand set in your hands and use your finger to hang up and get a

Chapter 5
Sales and Selling

new dial tone. It is easy to procrastinate while telemarketing, this is a good way to stop it. The first few times may be a bit rocky, but it will get easier and it will prove profitable.

Sources for lists to use can be your guest histories, comment cards (it is wise to ask them on the card if their company travels to your area often), trade associations, the Convention and Visitors' Bureau, Chamber of Commerce, trade journals and trade periodicals. Your employees may also be a source. If all else fails, you can create your own list of leads. Contact your library, Chamber of Commerce and phone books to find local business you feel can use your product. It all starts with a phone call.

One of my favorite techniques in finding leads with the telephone is the *travel agent call back*. The idea is to look at your arrivals list each morning. Note all the arrivals where the reservation was made by a travel agent. Call the agency and ask to speak to the person who made the individual reservation. When they come on the line, let them know you are expecting Mr. So-and-so and thank them for using your property. Check with them to make certain everything is accurate for this reservation. Finally, ask them if they have other travel coming into your area and see if you can accommodate that as well. The whole call may go something like this:

> You: **This is Joe with Bayside View Inn in San Francisco. Can I speak with the agent responsible for a reservation I have for Mr. Doyle checking in today.**

When speaking with the appropriate agent: This is Joe with the Bayside View Inn in San Francisco. We are expecting Mr. Doyle to check-in today. I am calling to thank you for using our property. We really appreciate your business. Is there anything special I should be aware of regarding Mr. Doyle?

Agent: Yes, make certain that he gets a non-smoking room. Also, he won't be arriving till after nine tonight.

You: Fine, we will hold his room for a late check-in. It looks like he is with Amalgamated Plastic and Metals, do they travel to San Francisco often?

Agent: Yes, but they always stay at the Beach and Bridge Motel. They were full so I thought I would put him with your property.

You: Thank you for giving us the opportunity...

Now you uncover all the needs that that agent has for Amalgamated Plastics and Metals so you can host *all* their travel into the area. This is a very unobtrusive way to make a sales call and you are speaking with people who already are using your property. The idea is to see if they have more travel you can accommodate. It is also good to ask if they work for any other companies that come into your area.

Actively network. Apart from keeping your mind open to new ideas, attending programs is a great way to

Chapter 5
Sales and Selling

network. **(Keep in mind it is very difficult to network from your living room, so get out there!)** When you do attend a function, make it worth your while. Arrive 15 minutes early and stay 15 minutes after the program is over. Meet people. People often say the problems they encounter with networking is they never know what to talk about. Well, here is a solid answer, ask them what business they are in and ask how they go about finding new business. This will do two things. First, you will have started a conversation with a total stranger. After you establish some sort of rapport you can ask other questions. See if they have a need for your property. Secondly, you may find new ways you can market and sell your property.

Try to go to these networking functions alone. If you do take someone from work, split up and cover opposite sides of the room. Most likely you already know the person you brought, use this time to meet new people. Take plenty of business cards and ask others for theirs. Finally, if you cannot find networking functions to attend then take the responsibility and host an open house for your property and create a networking environment. Sometimes you just have to do things yourself.

Get outside! Like I mentioned before, you will not drum up any business by hiding in your office. If your getting burnt out making calls or writing letters, then get out of the office and visit the businesses in your area and *find leads.* At least you'll be moving and you certainly wont fill rooms by being stagnant. Remember that you may be on the right track but you'll get run over if you just sit there.

Everyone that you come in contact with either can use your property themselves or has contact with someone who can use your property. They themselves may need guest rooms some day. Their family and friends may need your property. The people they work with could be looking for rooms or the company they work for may have people coming into your area. Additionally, the clubs and organizations they belong to may accommodate speakers and other travelers. Don't underestimate the influence someone can have on your property.

Speaking with Clients

Whether on the phone, on a sales presentation or networking in a social situation you must be cognizant of the way you come across to people. You must fine tune the way you communicate. A pitfall encountered by many owners and entrepreneurs is they have a great deal of pride for their product and they think that everyone should feel the same way. Different things are important to different people. It is your job to uncover the important items to address before you start into your well oiled presentation.

Communication is not talking so much as it is listening and intelligently reacting to the data received. Listening will give you much more information. When you speak with clients and potential guests use questions to uncover needed information regarding their needs. Always speak to people in their language and use expressions and verbiage they are likely to use and understand. After asking a question many people

Chapter 5
Sales and Selling

fail to shut up and *listen* to the answer. Don't make this mistake.

Great sales people have perfected their ability to *empathize* with others. They can put themselves in another person's shoes and relate to how that person feels. Empathy is important when building strong relationships. When selling your property to a potential user, empathize to show you understand what is important to them. A useful sentence is, "I understand why that is a concern," or simply, "I understand."

Sometimes new sales people will be doing everything in opposition to the techniques outlined in most sales books but they will be achieving the sales goals they have set. Usually all their success can be attributed to their enthusiasm and vitality. Many times these traits can compel a person to do business with you. Keep your enthusiasm high and join it with your deep product knowledge and your commitment to sharpening your sales skills. This is your winning formula.

> **They are able because they think they are able — Virgil.**

An important area to perfect in your presentations and sales techniques is to only speak in terms of the *benefit* to the client. Many people, when talking about their hotel or motel, dump all the features that their property has to offer on the poor person who agreed to listen. They will tell them all about the number of guest rooms, amenities offered, size of their pool, their AAA rating, and rates. This is called *feature dumping*.

There are two obvious dangers in this. First, the sales person is rattling off everything known about their property without first finding out what specific items are important to the client. It may be they couldn't give a lick about the size and capacity of your conference room which you spent ten minutes covering *thoroughly*, or worse, they may be directly opposed to using a property with any meeting space because of a bad experience at another property where their people were ignored because of an in-house group.

As a sales person, you should ask questions, lots of questions, to uncover the needs of the client. After you think you have uncovered a need, ask again if it is something that they are looking for. Confirm what you suspect. If after questioning the client will tell you that the counter space in the bathrooms of your competitor is very limited, you should ask them if their travelers need larger counter space. If yes, then you can tell her all about the extensive shelving you have recently installed in all the bathrooms. But remember, until you confirm she is looking for more counter space you should not continue. Why? Because what if she really enjoys the intimate space in the bathrooms of your competitor? What if she thinks that her travelers bring too many toiletries and she wants to limit their counter space? It may sound odd but you never know what their motivation is until you confirm. Granted you may have a good idea, but you don't want to open a can of worms when your trying to get her business. Focus on the customer, the guest or the client rather than the product you offer. This will force you to think in terms of what is important to them.

The second danger of feature dumping is that features do not motivate people to use your property. Benefits do. Clearasil doesn't sell acne medication, it sells clear skin. Black & Decker doesn't sell drill bits, they sell *holes*. Airport location isn't motivating for the client.

CHAPTER 5
SALES AND SELLING

The location is only a feature of the property. Put your features in terms of the benefit received. The airport location written as a benefit would be; Our airport location offers your travelers easy access after their long flight, they will not have to spend a grueling half hour cramped in a cab to get into the city and the cab fare they save can be used for something else. Benefits are the reasons people look for certain features. When you are speaking with someone, however, you will not want to leave it to them to translate your features into benefits. Do it for them and you may even create a need in their mind to start using your property.

> ➲With a sheet of paper list all the features that your property offers. Leave plenty of room between each. Next to each feature, list all the benefits you can. Be creative and tax your mind to create many. After you are finished go over this list again and again. You will want to have an excellent working knowledge of the appropriate benefits for each feature to use in your sales arsenal. When you uncover a need your property can satisfy, you should be able to recite the appropriate benefit in a confident and conversational manner.

The genuine upside to learning to present your property this way is you move away from the rate issue. Rate will always be a consideration and people always love paying less for something, but by moving intelligently through your presentation and discovering all the other items that are important you create a stronger argument to use your property. Studies have shown that rate, or price paid, is usually around number nine in the order of importance for staying at a hotel or motel. Use that to your advantage and sell security, cleanliness, location or what ever else happens to motivate the user. You will see offering discounted rates is not the only way you can get their commitment. Just remember to *word it as a benefit* and to make certain it is something they want to hear about.

In Person Sales Calls

The best way to get a commitment from someone to book your property, whether it be a travel agency, a tour operator or a company secretary, is to be in a face to face sales situation with that person. Because of this, you will want to schedule appointments and get out to see the people who can increase your occupancy. But before you are sitting in front of someone you will have to do a little homework.

If it is a company you are visiting, find out what it is they do. You will also want to know the name of the person you will be calling on and what it is they do. Just like you, these people are very busy and probably are not interested in filling you in on this information, especially when you want something from them. Be prepared; find this out in advance.

It is wise to spend some time anticipating what it is they will need from a lodging property and write down how it is your property can effectively meet those needs. Also consider any objections they will have about your property and decide how you will handle the objections.

Just as with telephone sales you will want to set your goals before you go in on a call. Put together a plan as to what information you want from the person you will be visiting and what action you want them to take. If you know of some group they are trying to place, maybe you will want to take the reservation while you are there. Maybe your goal is to get them to give you dates that you can check for availability. Possibly you can aim for their commitment to call you the next time they need a room. You will also want to have a backup plan in case things aren't going as you had envisioned.

While you are there, ask for referrals and leads. If you are visiting with someone currently using your property then you have a good chance at getting them to recommend someone they feel can also use your services. Your current clients are always good sources of leads.

Negotiating Rates

If you plan to pursue corporate volume, tour and travel or ad hoc group business you will be faced with the act of negotiating rates. People who are placing a large amount of business into your property will feel they deserve a discount off your rack rates. Remember "large amount of business" is a subjective term and your client will invariably feel that their definition of *large* is broad while yours will probably be more narrow.

Some of the people you will be working with will have their industry standards for what rates they require from a property for that property to be considered in their travel programs. Their policy may be worded ...*at least 50% off your quoted rack rate*. It is up to you to decide if your property would want this business. It will also be up to you to monitor their production (the amount of rooms they are actually placing into your property) and get on their back if production is lower than promised. If it is lower, then you may want to go back and re-negotiate the rates for the next rate period.

If you are negotiating rates with an ad hoc group or a corporate volume account, have in mind what you are able to do and how low you are prepared to go to secure that business. Many people feel they must negotiate *something* before they can make a commitment. They will usually attempt to negotiate the rate because it has not entered their mind to ask for anything else. If you feel this is the case, try showing them other things you can offer rather than lowering your rate. Ideas could be complimentary upgrades for all their travelers, complimentary continental breakfast or giving them a direct billing account with your property to make payment easier. Try to increase the perceived value before you resort to lowering your rate.

> **What costs little is little worth —**
> **Baltasar Gracián.**

Most often you will be asked to lower your rate. People like to get something for less, however they may not have any idea how much less they would like the rate to be. Often people subscribe to the **third proposed rate rule**.

> Third proposed rate rule: Accepting the third rate proposed from the lodging property sales manager when the rates are reduced with each proposal.

An example would be your first quote was $100 per room per night. The group planner doesn't accept this

Chapter 5
Sales and Selling

rate because it was the first one proposed and they would like to see if they can get it a little cheaper. They are thinking that it never hurts to ask, so they tell you it is too high. You quote them a second rate, a little lower than the first. They do not accept this one either because now they have learned you are willing to negotiate, so they tell you it is a little too high still. You propose a third quote. Stay firm with this one. In most cases they will accept it, even if they have to argue over it for a while.

> **It's unwise to pay too much, but it's unwise to pay too little. When you pay too much you loose a little money, that is all. When you pay too little you sometimes loose everything, because the thing you bought was incapable of doing the thing you bought it to do.**
>
> **The common law of business balance prohibits paying a little and getting a lot. It can't be done. If you deal with the lowest bidder, it's well to add something for the risk you run. And if you do that, you will have enough to pay for something better — John Ruskin (1819 - 1900).**

You can manipulate this rule to your favor. Keep in mind that in most rate negotiations if they tell you the first quote is too high you will probably have to quote two more. Instead of dropping your $100 rate to $85, then in turn to $70, keep your rate reductions smaller. Try $100, then $90, and then $85 and stay firm with $85 to see if they will come around and place the business. If you must lower the rate even more because their budget really cannot pay the $85, and you have decided at the onset you can go even lower, then you will want to reduce it again to accommodate the business. However, if they only wanted to wait for your third proposed rate then you are much better off with the $85 than discounting your rooms quickly and leaving money on the table.

Organizing Your Accounts

As you move through the sales and marketing process, turning your marketing into leads and your leads into clients, you will begin generating much account information and you will want to keep in organized so that you are focusing your sales time on the most appropriate client at that moment.

Keep a file for all the lists and articles you find that would be good for marketing your property. These are in the very initial stages of your effort and you are planning to contact them to see if they qualify as a lead you should be working on. After you contact them you will add the ones that qualify to the contact management system you have adopted. It may be a filing system or a computer software program. What ever it is you should be on top of the people that can use your property and try to increase the amount of business they give you. You should be in contact with every client at least once every three months. Some software programs will let you schedule this. If not, use a tickler card file that lets you file a card three months out to remind you to contact your important clients.

> Don't stand shivering on the bank; plunge in at once, and have it over — Sam Slick.

Some hotel sales people have adopted a grading system for each of their accounts that lets them know exactly

Chapter 5
Sales and Selling

what action would be most appropriate when the time comes to contact and how often that contact should be. It is a grading system where each account gets assigned a grade of A, B or C. The A accounts are the ones that have immediate need for your property or your area. They may be the accounts that are giving most or all of their room nights to a competitor, but fit the profile of someone who would use your property. These are accounts that obviously have business *now*. The B accounts could be those with a lesser amount of travel into your area than the A's, or they may not have the travel now but you know it will be coming up. The C's are the ones who seem to have a need for your services but you aren't certain yet. Nothing should remain a C for long. It should become an A or B. If they have no business then you kill that account.

You will want to create a grading system which is appropriate for your property and the type of clients you call on. With a grading system you can focus more in-person selling on the A accounts more often. The B's can be contacted by mail and the telephone more than in person. Account grading will help you to spend your valuable time wisely.

Chapter 6 Offering Exceptional Service for Repeat Business

Exceed Your Guests Expectations

This chapter on service is critical to an effective campaign to increase your revenue. Now that you are cognizant of who your potential guests are, you are probably becoming aware of the cost to attract them. In the end the cost should be justified by the increase in your bottom line. There is a marketable group which is relatively easy to contact and already has a need for your product. These are the guests who are currently staying in your establishment. In comparison to attracting new business, it is relatively inexpensive to market to them. But the value must be there the first time they stay in order for them to accept your offer to return. The level of service you

> Lots of folks confuse bad management with destiny. — Kin Hubbard

provide will shape their desire to return. Exceed their expectations and you can master their loyalty.

Ray Kroc, the founder of the modern fast food industry, took McDonald's to before undreamed of heights as a symbol of Americana the world over. And a place to get a decent hamburger, whether in Pittsburg or Paris. He turned McDonald's into an institution because of two things; the uniformity and the consistency you will find at *all* McDonald's restaurants. The credo of McDonald's is on the wall of each and every restaurant; Quality, Service, Cleanliness and Value (QSCV). This is the focus of each restaurant and has become a benchmark for the entire hospitality industry. Adopt QSCV in your operation and you can create repeat business like the mammoth fast food chain.

Excellent service is the catalyst to generate your repeat guest business. There is a lot of competition for room sales. Be persistent with the guests you have. By serving them above their expectations you may even add to your positive word of mouth advertising.

There is a relationship between price and value. As long as people feel that the services received can justify the price, they will pay. The common denominator of you and all your competition (your competition can even include the friends and relatives people opt to stay with rather than paying for lodging) is that everyone is offering a room; shelter, warmth and, to a degree, security. But rates greatly fluctuate to cover all segments of the market. What justifies the rate tiers is the level of service offered — higher service usually equivocates higher rate — and if the equation balances there should be someone available to pay that rate. The key is to position your property and its services to attract the largest portion of demand for your area at the highest rate. Remember long after the trip is over, people will remember the quality of service and what was received before they will remember the rate paid. Keeping this in mind you may want to reevaluate the tangible services and amenities you offer, possibly upgrading them, and adjust the room rate.

Amenities

Amenities are the extras that you offer and are included in the room rate. One of the most popular with travelers is the complimentary breakfast. More than any other meal, breakfast is the one travelers will use most in the lodging facility. If you offer complimentary full or continental breakfast, use this strong point to attract a greater share of volume corporate business. Make it known during your sales presentation and let those with the potential to book your property understand this could be important to them. Other amenities that show your attention to detail could be in-room coffee machines, morning newspapers, and complimentary evening wine reception in the lobby.

You may want to consider special amenities for your VIP guests. Most likely, these guests will have the ability to influence the travel decisions of others who come into your area. They could be travel agents, tour operators, employees from a local attraction or a frequent business traveler. Consider putting together something special for them to find in their room. A bottle of wine, flowers, upgraded bathing products and candy are all appreciated. Often a welcome note from the owner or manager that lets them know you are available should they have any special needs will begin their stay on a positive note.

By sending something special to their room you are telling them you want and appreciate their business and you will, in turn, take good care of anyone they send there. You are letting them know they can rest assured while recommending your property to family, friends and colleagues. Also if they are exceptionally important to you, call them in their room after they check in to see if all is well and if they are in need of anything. Let them know you are the owner/General Manager/Director of Sales and you want to insure they have a great stay.

Basics

There are certain basic areas you must cover in regard to service. People expect certain things in exchange for the rate paid. When these expectations are met you will receive no special consideration from the guest. You have only met their expectations. However, if any of these basic service issues are overlooked you will most likely seriously disappoint the guest.

The first and foremost is neatness and cleanliness. These are important. Dress for work, even if you live on the premises. Every person that has the potential of guest contact should be well dressed. Keep the front desk, and any area a guest may see, professional. The lobby and front desk area is the first impression people have and it will give them an indication of what to expect in the rooms. Don't give them the opportunity to change their mind about staying with you because of the way you keep the front areas. They should be in order and clean. Not only should they look clean, they should *smell* clean.

The decor of the front area should be attractive and inviting. This sets the tone for your property and the guest rooms. Make certain that it makes for a good impression.

Always smile, even when talking on the phone (people can feel it on the other end of the line). It is contagious. Besides, your business is hospitality. Remember the guests have no obligation to stay with you. Never treat them as if they are an inconvenience.

It may be a wise idea, if you have many people on your staff that come into contact with guests, to set up standards for performance you expect from each employee. This way you are able to control and somewhat ensure a certain level of personableness and guest satisfaction. The following is a good list to start with. Let your staff know how important these are to you and work with them to implement their use. Remember all the problems and successes reflect on management. Take responsibility for your employees service education.

- ♦ Always make eye contact with guests,
- ♦ When on the phone, acknowledge guests that are waiting. Sometimes a friendly nod of your head will be enough,
- ♦ Keep a sense of immediacy when attending to a guests request,
- ♦ Keep the guest updated as to your progress in servicing them,
- ♦ Attend to guests who seem in need of assistance,

- Always excuse yourself if you have to leave a guest,
- Never criticize anyone if front of a guest,
- Never criticize a guest,
- Attend to complaints immediately, and
- Use peoples' names.

The list you devise should reflect the work environment particular to your property. By establishing service standards you bring yourself closer to offering your guests consistency, something important to repeat clientele.

Telephone demeanor should be helpful, polite, and courteous. This is usually the first contact a guest has with your property, and can shape his or her entire vision of your establishment. Identify your property clearly when answering the phone. You may also want to give your name as well. Take the time to practice your telephone skills and make certain that anyone who may be answering the phone is aware of your high expectations. Implement standard procedures for you and your staff when on the phone. These should include never placing someone on hold without first asking their permission. Check back with them after a minute if you must be longer and let them know how long you think you will be. Offer to call them back. Be as service oriented as possible and you will win the loyalty of your guests.

In your focus to be service oriented you should look at the method of payments you currently accept. If you do not accept credit cards, you should. Otherwise you are not meeting your guests basic expectations. Credit cards are a fact of life today, and their use will only increase. If you are not accepting them you are most likely turning away business, possibly preventing guests from staying one extra night and preventing any chance of a guest returning in the future. Accept them gladly. It makes payment easier and people that are traveling probably do not feel comfortable carrying lots of cash.

If you want to increase your business from travel agents, corporate travel offices or small companies in feeder markets, make it easy for them to make the reservation. Consider providing a toll free number. It is another side of your service focus and a way of showing these companies that you invite their business. Unless you have the number on the brochure, only the people you give it to will use it. You are able to control this if you prefer.

In addition to your toll free reservations line, you may want to consider having a private line installed. This can be impressive if you are actively soliciting the incoming travel of local businesses. If you are the owner or manager it is particularly impressive to give your "private line" number so they may make their reservation directly with you, rather than to call the front desk. This can make them feel that they are of special importance to you and they can also feel secure that by making the reservation through you it will get your utmost attention.

> **The great advantage of a hotel is that it's a refuge from home life.**
> **— George Bernard Shaw**

Make certain the people who will answer this private line greet the caller with something to identify it as your office, such as, "Mr./Ms. Venable's office." Make it seem you are giving these important clients a way to bypass the conventional route to make the reservation. If you are unable to take the call at that time, remember to return the call. If you fail to do this, your private line has only become another frustration for the person trying to make a reservation.

A simple way to ease your guests out of their daily frustrations and to increase your repeat business is to use their name when speaking with them. Ethel Nada, the General Manager of the Breakers Hotel in Honolulu, Hawaii, is an expert at this. She consistently greets me and my guests by our names when she sees us on property. She does this with most of the guests but everyone feels special and even a little important that the GM is greeting them by their name. (She is also very effective in her use of her database, I receive a holiday/Christmas post card from her every December.) Being recognized by any member of the staff can increase your guests' loyalty. Every guest has to provide their name at check-in, and so often the staff doesn't use it. In the hectic business climate of today's world it doesn't happen often. Use this to your advantage and use their names. They will remember you for it.

Comment Cards and Complaints

Providing comment cards is a great tool to get guests' feedback, however, they are rarely filled out. Have your desk clerks ask the guests to fill them out as they are checking out. If they are in a rush the desk clerk can hand them an addressed and stamped envelope so the guest can easily drop it in the mail at their convenience. If time is really pressed, the very least the desk clerk can do is to ask what could be done to make their stay more enjoyable. The comment card is one of the best ways to be alerted to repairs that are needed in the rooms.

If a guest fills out a comment card and is very critical, do not delay, rectify the problem and call the guest back. It is an easy process to calm someone down over the telephone. Let them know you appreciate their input and the problem has been solved. Invite more critique and be prepared to take it. Listening to a complaint is a form of market research. By showing you listen and care the guest will feel closer to you and your property and are more likely to return. Invite them back. The comment card gives you an opportunity to turn a negative experience into a positive one. Whereas without the negative experience their stay could have been fine but they would have felt no loyalty to return, now they have been part of the process to make your property better, they have gotten to know you better and they feel genuinely good about it. They are also aware of what is important to you; their satisfaction. Highlight these words; <u>you can make people loyal</u>. The guest may be wrong, but they are right in any sort of dispute. Just exceed their expectations and they will return for more.

You may also have the opportunity to handle a complaint while the guest is on property. These complaints should be handled promptly. Even if you get a complaint of something you have already rectified, contact the guest and let them know you appreciate their input and help and you have done something about it. This will help you to maintain your credibility.

If the complaint comes in over the phone, take the call then. Do not opt to call them back, you have an opportunity to solve the problem immediately *and at their expense*. Let the person calling understand that you guarantee to work through the problem to their satisfaction. Ask the customer what resolution they are looking for before you suggest a solution. What they have in mind is usually easier and not as expensive as what you would have proposed. Many times they just want their story to be heard and acknowledged.

Those Who Book Your Property

Pay your travel agent commissions promptly. You not only need to provide service to your guests but also to those who represent your guests. You want their repeat business too. For some properties, travel agents are the life blood. Treat them extra special and let them know you appreciate their using your property. A hotel in Denver sends out the scratcher lottery tickets with the commission checks. They agents love it and it becomes an incentive to further book the property. Of course, they see that each reservation could net them a million dollars! Commission checks should be sent out within 48 hours of the guests' departure. The agents should not have to wait. They have provided their service, don't delay in paying them.

When accommodating groups, pay close attention to all the details in making them feel welcome and to encourage their repeat business. It is a solid idea to assign one staff member to be the groups' liaison to your property during their stay. This should make it easier on the group to get their needs satisfied. Put together a book of all the relevant phone numbers and services, such as translation services, tourist offices, consulates, attractions and the like. Be sure to include things like the AT&T on line translation service that you can use with your phone. This book can serve as a mobile concierge. With the information you put together your liaison will be well prepared for most anything, and your sleek and efficient operation will attract the attention of the group members who can be repeat guests, as well as the group leader.

It is especially important for your liaison and the entire property to be sympathetic to your group bookings' special needs. Repeat group business is a smart way to lay a solid foundation of reservations on which to build. Exploit every opportunity for them to return.

Chapter 7 Assigning the Right Objectives, Strategies and Tactics to Your Plan

Your Research Develops Into Your Plan

Your involvement in this book thus far has been strictly research. You have collected data on your property, your competition, and the market. You also should have many ideas of how to sell, market and promote a

| Genius borrows nobly. |
| — Ralph Waldo Emerson |

lodging property. Because each property is unique, and in many cases *extremely* unique, not all of what you have read can apply to every property. It is still valuable to know the various avenues that have been explored in relation to all types of hotel and motel sales and marketing. Hopefully you were able to adjust some of the ideas of the previous chapters to work for your particular instance.

In this chapter you will put to paper the objectives that you wish to achieve for your property in regards to; revenue production, average rate, occupancy, and revPAR. The following chapter will involve your action plan. In that chapter you will break down your objectives into small, measurable steps (called action steps) by each day of the year. Your Sales and Marketing Plan will be a guide and a benchmark. Every decision you will make in the next twelve months will have to be justified against your Sales and Marketing Plan. This is to keep your property on the straight and narrow, leading you to a focused and final goal. For all other purposes, i.e. your day to day activities, you will refer to your action plan. Because you have broken the objectives of your Sales and Marketing Plan into day by day action steps, you can release the stress of the process and rest assured in the successful completion of your plan. If every day you live is successful, i.e. you complete each point on your action plan for that day, then eventually you will have a successful year. It is unavoidable if you do it this way. Let's get started in putting together an achievable Sales and Marketing Plan.

The Reasons Some Plans Do Not Succeed

Planner/property changes direction mid-stream. Well meaning people often put together and start on a plan, only to change direction mid-stream. This will only lead to a weakened sales effort and probably negative impact to your outlined objectives. The failure rate for lodging property marketing plans is for the most part, not attributed to any integral flaw in the program, but rather that the action steps were not properly delegated. You must commit to see your plans through to the end. Only then can you determine whether your efforts were effective. Most likely, the efforts will prove to be effective and your final critique will show ways that the effectiveness can be even greater.

Plan not incorporated into daily activities. One of the main reasons plans fail is once the Sales and Marketing Plan has been completed the creator fails to incorporate it into the daily activities of himself/herself, the managers and employees. This is overcome by the creation of the action plan and writing those action steps into your day calendar so they become part of your daily to-do lists.

Results are expected in the short term. Another reason is this cannot be viewed as a short term investment. There will be no big payoff for the dollars and time invested in the first few months. You have to be committed to this for the long haul and be secure in the daily successes and that they will bring their natural reward. You get out of it what you put in, even more. The sum will be a synergetic relationship, whereas the total is greater than what the individual parts can achieve. It is sometimes called the snowball effect. Your efforts will one day payoff more than the cost of the investment.

Planner assumes that financial projections can act as a plan. The projections the planner has made only act as a basis for the objectives. These objectives will be your property's *raison d'être* for the coming twelve months. The financial projections will not tell you how to achieve them. They are only your goals (but only if written down, more on this later), a snapshot of the end of the road and not the map of how to get there.

Planner has not interpreted the data correctly. The data you collected on your property, your competition and the market can tell you a lot, but you have to be realistic. Many times the creator of a Sales and Marketing Plan has been too lofty in his/her predictions or has been quick to jump to conclusions regarding the data. Take the time to interpret the data in a methodical manner. Create if/then scenarios to arrive at the best plan of action. Only with your objectives grounded in fact can you plan a way to achieve them.

The Mission Statement

A mission statement is a short tenet, usually one sentence, giving the reason why your company exists. Business professionals use this as the guide from which all business decisions should be made. It is the answer to the question, "what business am I/are we in?" If everything you do is in line and agreement with your mission statement then your property should be on the right track.

> ➲Create a mission statement for your business. Put into one or two sentences the type of business you are in and its purpose. This will serve as your guide in creating your Sales and Marketing Plan.

Preparing Objectives

The Sales and Marketing Plan you create should become a tool you can put to good use. Often larger hotels prepare a behemoth stack of paper, call it the marketing plan and never look at it again during the course of the year. These plans are crippling. They should never waste the time to prepare something they wont use or follow (They prepare these primarily for the investors so the hotel may show them the sales department has direction).

It wont do you any good to just compile a lot of statistical data, package it in order and put it aside. If it is accurate and has meaning you will trust it to guide you to greater profitability. Because you are an operator with daily contact with your property, you need to create a plan with direction and economy. Something to refer to, chart progress and claim the results as they happen. There really is a golden rule to the universe; your efforts

> One can never consent to creep when one feels an impulse to soar.
> — Helen Keller

will be rewarded. By taking the time now to map out a plan you can stack the odds that you efforts are rewarded by increased revenue rather than lessons learned. For your plan to be effective it must be concise, organized and to the point. This is *your* map. You are not writing this for a grade in composition. Keep it simple and useable, but be precise.

The objectives you will write in your Sales and Marketing Plan are simply your goals. For any type of goal to be effective it must have four characteristics:

It must be measurable. "I want to increase my total revenue" is not a goal. How will you know when it has been successfully completed? Better yet, how will you know if you are making progress and how much? Give yourself a figure. "I want to increase revenue by $50,000 in the next twelve months over the last twelve months" is much more focused. It is a goal. When you do increase your revenue by that amount you can cross it off your list and know without a doubt you were successful.

It must have a date of completion. In the example above the date of completion is at the end of twelve months. Without deciding on a date of completion you will not have the sense of urgency to get going, you will not have a way to check your progress within a time frame and you will not have committed completely to the goal.

It must be believable. Hopefully by now your analysis has given you a realistic picture of where you plan to take your property. A goal to become a first class vacation resort with a ten unit motel on the intersection of the 5 and the 10 freeways in LA is too much of a stretch of the imagination, even for Hollywood. If your goal is not believable, you will loose interest. There is a fine line to tread; it has to be a little better than you best — this is to force you to strive to do better — and it also has to be within your reach. Make it believable and it will be achievable.

It must be written down. Luckily we are in the process of taking care of that. If it is not written down in black and white then it is not a goal, it is merely a wish, a desire. With all the goals in your life, *write them down.* You will be amazed at what will be accomplished after you commit it to paper.

Chapter 7 Assigning The Right Objectives, Strategies and Tactics to Your Plan

Keep in mind that as you went through your history and forecasting, you may have come to realize the year ahead is going to be very lean. You may have realized that before and that is the reason you are reading this book. If you are aware it will be difficult to achieve the status quo or match your revenue for last year remember it is acceptable to have goals that are not an *increase* in revenue, occupancy, ADR or revPAR. Don't allow yourself to loose site of the forest for the trees by attempting monumental performance increases during periods of an adverse hospitality market. Look at the early 90's. These were times when everyone's goal was to stay above water and survive. In fact, "survive till '95" was the slogan of many sales departments.

You will create four main objectives for your property. They will refer to you occupancy, ADR, revenue and revPAR. You may have these objectives for a one year period if your business is steady year round. Chances are that it is not. Consider how your business is influenced and its response and set your objectives' time frame in the appropriate manner. For example, if there is a seasonal slant to your occupancies I would suggest quarterly, or even monthly, objectives. Because you are deciding on the time frame now, it will be easier to evaluate the effectiveness of your objective plan.

In chapter two you spent much time and effort evaluating the total demand for accommodations for you and your competition, and any changes you anticipate to this demand. You looked at your current market penetration and your ability to out perform your competition. You have identified and anticipated change to the supply of rooms in your area. Now, use this information to set realistic objectives for your property. Take it all into consideration as you set your four main objectives.

> ➲Take out a sheet of paper and write out the main objectives you want to attain. Be certain to write them as measurable, believable and with a date of completion. Most likely your date of completion will be one year away, but you may want to include measurable performance checks along the way, either quarterly or monthly.
>
> After you have listed all four, take you first objective. List the strategies that will achieve your performance objectives. With each of these strategies you will list the tactics that fill out the strategy.

You may also want to consider having strategies pertaining to the amount of reservations you will have on the books for the following year and their placement, i.e. to have 10% of room reservations filled for the February, 12% for March, 8% for April... for the following year. If it is applicable business for your property, this type of strategy will force you to focus your sales effort toward more long term group business and tour groups. Other ideas for strategies can include:

- Obtain two new volume accounts giving at least 200 room nights each year,
- Booking one extra tour bus group each month,
- Increasing the score on the guest room survey cards by two points, and
- Shifting the market mix to 60% corporate guests.

It may seem a bit complicated and overwhelming but consider this example. Your objective is to increase this year's annual revenue by $20,000 over last year's. (Note: The objective is measurable, assumed to be believable, and the date of completion is the end of the calendar year.) The strategies you list that will bring about this achievement could be these two; increase the occupancy by 7% over last year and increase ADR by $7.85 over last year. Assuming you have a 100 unit property this will fulfill your objective.

With those two strategies you will list the tactics, or the actual steps you will take to implement a strategy. The tactics for the strategy of 7% increase in occupancy will be taken from much of the market analysis. It may be the following:

- To shift your market mix of tour group business to a larger share of the pie,
- Use forecasting to move business into need and shoulder periods (letting the high demand periods take care of themselves) by asking the reservation call for potentially impacted dates if their dates are flexible, and
- Perform x number of sales calls per week to area corporate business to increase Monday through Thursday traffic.

The tactics become the area where you add meat to marketing plan and these are the points that will construct your action plan. Share your strategies with some employees. Have them brainstorm tactics to implement them. You may find new ideas when you ask the assistance of others.

You should consider including one tactic of *networking to uncover new business*. If you strategy was to increase rate then you can network to uncover higher rated business. If it was to increase occupancy, then you can network to get more business. I urge you to take advantage of all the Chamber mixers, associations that you are a member (Kiwanis, Lions, Rotary, Altrusa, etc.), and community business groups. They can offer you many contacts, support and opportunities for increased business. It may be difficult to see exactly how these networking functions can impact your objective in the sense of attempting to assign a value (measurable) to each event attended. However, these are where you will uncover gold, find leads and practice your skills as a sales person.

Chapter 8 Action Plan: Breaking Everything Down Into Small Steps

Your Action Plan Defined

The action plan is the mechanical part of creating the total Sales and Marketing Plan for your property. It's purpose is to identify all the individual steps you outlined in the tactics in the last chapter and your promotional strategy from chapter four and map them out, day by day, to bring the entire program to fruition. Your action plan is nothing more than a calendar filled in with the initiatives to be taken to achieve the objectives outlined.

> We consume our tomorrows fretting about our yesterdays. — Persius

Comfort in Security

By breaking these things down to the smallest task you can insure each is done successfully with minimal effort. These small steps will be less monumental, ideally they will appear painless, and you will not be wondering what it is you should be doing next. Your action plan will tell you with certainty the next item to be completed.

A successful year is broken down to twelve successful months, each one being nothing more than four successful weeks, each of those being nothing more than seven successful days. Live each day successfully and eventually you will have a successful year. If you think about it, if you can go to bed each night knowing that your day was successful, and are able to do this with each day, then you should never have to worry. Your year will ultimately be successful. All you need is to plan thoroughly, then put the plan aside and live each day successfully. To do this you will refer to your action plan.

It was said that, basically, your action plan is your calendar; your Daytimer, Franklin Planner, Filofax, whatever. For the purposes of creating the action plan, it is suggested to photocopy a standard monthly calendar and fill in the dates. When completed this will be part of the Sales and Marketing Plan. After that you should transfer all the information into whatever daily planner you use. The reason you should start with the standard monthly calendar and include it in the Sales and Marketing Plan is so it will be accessible to whoever wishes to check the progress of the plan. The reason for transferring the information into your daily

CHAPTER 8 ACTION PLAN: BREAKING EVERYTHING DOWN INTO SMALL STEPS 147

planner is that way it will not be overlooked. You will have incorporated these actions into all the other things you will have scheduled for yourself. It has been learned that the people who achieve most in their days are the people who keep one planner and incorporate business and personal life in that planner.

⬥Find a standard monthly calendar, the type where each sheet is a different month with big squares for each day. You can even make one with sheets of 8 1/2" x 11" paper, a pencil and a ruler. Refer to the first objective you set. Analyze the strategies and the tactics. Now, assign dates to the individual tasks that need to be performed. Start with one and work through the entire year before you look at the next one. For example, if you are doing a quarterly newsletter to selected travel agencies you may insert the following into your yearly calendar:

Dec. 10, 1997 Complete address list for newsletter mailing group.

Dec. 15, 1997 Enter address list into database.

Dec. 26, 1997 Prepare first quarter newsletter.

Jan. 2, 1998 Print and mail newsletter.

Mar. 15, 1998 Prepare second quarter newsletter.

Apr. 2, 1998 Print and mail newsletter.

Jun. 15, 1998   Prepare third quarter newsletter.

Jul. 2, 1998   Print and mail newsletter.

Sep. 15, 1998   Prepare fourth quarter newsletter.

Oct. 2, 1998   Print and mail newsletter.

If you were to also plan to send them holiday cards you would probably put a date on your calendar in October to order them, another date in November to address, sign and stuff envelopes and a mailing date at the beginning of December. This may seem a bit tedious, but the point is to map it out, step by step, and then forget it (figuratively). This way everything is certain to get done and nothing will be forgotten (literally).

If you had planned three outside sales calls every Tuesday morning then fill that in on *every appropriate* Tuesday in your calendar (you wouldn't fill out a holiday like Christmas if it fell on a Tuesday). You will want to write in all the networking functions for the year.

> He who hesitates is last. — Mae West

Most likely the Chamber of Commerce has some monthly mixer, possibly your Convention and Visitors' Bureau will have evenings or lunches lined up during the year. Try to attend as many as you can. This is the time to write in all the trade shows or conventions you plan to attend and set aside dates for any business trips and dates for telemarketing.

Continue to do this till every tactic is accounted for. This is your action plan. It really is simple, but then again, most of life's truths are simple. There is no real secret to being a successful lodging property. It takes creativity, hard work, organization and commitment. This commitment is not only to your Sales and Marketing Plan but also to the learning process.

After you finish putting together the final Sales and Marketing Plan, remember to come back to the action plan and transfer the dates and initiatives to your personal daily planner. If you don't currently use one, this is a good time to start. It will maximize the effectiveness of your marketing program and will help you be a sales professional.

Chapter 9 Budgeting

When to Set Your Budget

I have placed the chapter on budgeting at the end of the book. Contrary to the past views of the hotel industry, it also belongs at the end of the planning process. If you spend promotional dollars and there is no positive impact to your property then your dollars are wasted. You would have been better off financially had you had done nothing. That is the reason your research is so important. The analysis you have prepared, if interpreted intelligently, should tell you in which areas to spend your marketing dollars.

Some of your promotion will be close to free. Press releases and in-house promotions are good examples and if done properly and creatively, they should perform their intended task; to get your reservation's line to ring. But obviously there is a good part of your marketing effort that will not be free. You must think of the cost of marketing as an *investment*. Because you have complete control over your marketing effort, you can fine tune the cost of each action step for its greatest return. When you spend marketing dollars wisely you are investing in your property and its future.

Adopt the Task Approach

There are as many marketing budgets as there are hotels and most follow a *percentage of sales* approach to budgeting. With this approach, management assumes that the budget (investment) for marketing is best arrived at by a fixed percentage of rooms gross income. Sometimes this is taken from the projected gross income; what you have forecasted to achieve. Most often, the budget is arrived by using the previous year's sales. For many properties this percentage falls from 3.5% up to 8%. Obviously this variance in percentage of gross income has to do with the economy and the type of property in question. Although this approach has no logical basis, it can only be somewhat effective for those properties that have a large amount of repeat business and where business is fairly steady year after year.

> You have to spend money to make money — American Proverb.

Another approach used by many is the *competitive parity* approach. With this approach an operator budgets in relation to the budgets set by the competition. Even if the competition had budgeted effectively, it is no guarantee that it would perform for your property.

Chapter 9
Budgeting

I discourage you form using either of these approaches. The core concept of preparing a marketing strategy is that there is an algebraic relationship which states if one performs x then the revenue will increase by y. To perform x there is a cost involved. All the previous chapters have helped you to identify the specific things which will actually impact your occupancy, rate, revPAR, yield statistic and market mix.

A logical and appropriate approach to budgeting monies is to justify each expense outlined in your action plan and assign the dollar amount necessary to get each job done. This is called the *task budgeting* or *zero base* approach. I urge you to use it. Task budgeting forces you to question every expenditure as opposed to determining a budget amount and then deciding how to allocate the funds. Like I stated earlier in this chapter, you should assign your budget *after* you have identified all the tasks which are required to achieve your objectives. These tasks are listed point by point in your objectives, strategies and tactics.

> ➲Next to each of the tactics listed, estimate the cost of performing it. Cost it out thoroughly and completely. Take into consideration every last detail. If you are estimating the cost of your quarterly newsletters you will first consider the size of the mailing list. This is the number of newsletters you will send every three months (four times a year). Take the size of you mailing and multiply it by four (number of people you will mail to times the number of times you will mail this year). Remember you will need one envelope, one letter, one stamp and one business card for

each. You will cost this into the amount you assign for the task. Also, will you be purchasing new computer software? Will you be renting a mailing list (if you do you will have to rent it each time you use it)? Figure the cost of any new brochures, stationary or other printed material that you plan to order in the next twelve months. Make certain you cover all costs regarding payroll (will you be hiring extra help?), dues for associations, collateral pieces, operating expenses, sales calls, specialty advertising, amenities and give-away items.

After you have estimated the true cost of all you plan to do, you will sum this to arrive at your annual budget. You know your property better than anyone else so look at this budget carefully. If it is necessary to reduce that figure then reevaluate the *entire* program and delete only those tasks that will not effect your overall objective first.

This task approach to budgeting can be viewed as a *bottom-up* method. Although it will require much more effort than one of the other approaches, it will force you to carefully consider the estimated benefit of each task and hold it against the investment. It also leads you to a very detailed marketing plan because in order to arrive at the yearly budget you must plan the entire year, day by day. Because of your methodic analysis your marketing plan should give you a positive return on the investment. You know well in advance what to expect and have an estimated cost. This will give you the justification for your future tasks you will

> **Nobody ever lost money taking a profit — Bernard Baruch.**

undertake. The task approach is very appropriate for properties just beginning a marketing program.

Chapter 10 Sales and Marketing Plan

You Have Made It

Congratulations on making it! You have the meat of your Sales and Marketing Plan. The rest of the assembly is cosmetic, however your work is just beginning. After the assembly is complete you will dive head long into implementing your plan into your daily life and the daily activities of your staff. Every plan will be slightly different as you adapt it for the integral circumstances of your property. With all this research, analysis and if/then scenarios you have become an erudite concerning your property and the realistic marketing options available to you. I hope you have created an exciting map for your journey and you have been a little daring with your creativity. No one ever

> **Patience is a necessary ingredient of genius —
> Benjamin Disrael.**

got very far by standing still; there is always something to gain by stretching yourself in new directions.

What You Have Accomplished

The analysis you completed in chapter two forced you to think of your property and your competition in quantitative and qualitative terms. When you compared them with the available markets you were able to see which ones you could attract and may have considered some repositioning for your property.

The historical information showed you high demand periods, as well as need periods and shoulder periods. This gave you insight as to what to expect next year and which dates you may want to focus some of your sales effort. It may have showed you where you can increase revenue through higher rate quotes and where you can increase occupancy by moving business. From this you created your next year's forecast of occupancy and rates for each of the 365 days.

The analysis of the market should have demonstrated how your market mix currently looks and what you hope it could be. You may have been introduced to markets you hadn't before considered for your property.

All of these items came early in the book to lay the ground work for setting your definite objectives and attaching to them their strategies and tactics. You will include all this work at the front of your Sales and Marketing Plan. As you move through the action steps you may want to consult these works if the steps are ever in need of fine tuning. They are also handy to refer

Chapter 10
Sales and Marketing Plan

to when you create the following year's Sales and Marketing Plan.

You put your objectives into writing to make your commitment to achieve them. Your objectives are based on the analysis you prepared. The strategies and tactics that will make you fulfill the individual objectives are the ideas you have come up with, and hopefully some that you found in the pages of this book, in terms of your sales and marketing effort.

The Promotional Strategy is included next. Remember that the inherent feature of this Promotional Strategy is that the effects are viewed in the long term and are less quantitative than your objectives. Much of the Promotional Strategy is based on your gut

> **Everything comes to him who hustles as he waits — Thomas Edison.**

instinct and intuition to determine the best moves for your property. The key to your Promotional Strategy is to generate inquiry and interest. It is 100% marketing.

The action plan outlines your day to day activities regarding your tactics and those tasks necessary in your Promotional Strategy. The action plan will be your most referred to section of the total plan. Make certain it is specific and clear. You cannot itemize too much in this area. Everything should be broken down to its *smallest step*. This is how the overall plan becomes bearable, believable, budgetable and *do-able*.

Your budget comes at the end. It should also be spelled out item by item, accounted for, and then this section can be placed aside (I am speaking figuratively, please keep it in the binder with the rest of the Sales and

Marketing Plan). You have the comfort in knowing everything that must be done, will get done without having to wonder where the money will come from or if this particular item is worth the investment. You have decided that it is worth the investment up front.

➡Get a three ring binder with identifying tabs and compile your Sales and Marketing Plan. I have put together the following outline for your plan but please assemble it in whatever way seems most appropriate for you. If you're like me, much of what you wrote throughout this book is far from legible. You may want to go back and copy some things so that it is neat and you can understand it.

This is *your* plan. You are not required to type it or make anything fancy, just as long as you can use it. The interpreted data and how you planned to use it is the important thing. Don't spend a lot of time making it presentable. You can better use your free time exploring other sales and marketing books, practicing your sales techniques or getting out there and making the contacts and the sales calls. After you compile your plan you are expected to live it. Your plan may be put together like this example.

Sales and Marketing Plan Assembly

- Analysis of your property
- Analysis of your competition
- Analysis of the market

- Historical information, previous year
  - Rate
  - Occupancy
  - RevPAR
  - Current market mix
- Forecasted information, coming year
  - Rates
  - Occupancy
  - RevPAR
  - Forecasted market mix
- Performance objectives
  - Strategies
  - Tactics
- Promotional Strategy
- Action plan
- Budget

Monitoring Your Plan

Your marketing program is for the long term. Measure the successes and grade the plan. You will use this information to adjust it the following year. Be careful not to abort your carefully mapped out program until you are absolutely certain you have given it adequate time to grow and demonstrate its effectiveness. You have given this a lot of thought and there should be little reason for anything less than success. It can be more costly to abort a plan because of your desire for immediate results. Be diligent and committed. The results should come with time. If you have given proper attention to the analysis and planning process then your program should be nothing short of excellent.

Because of all the effort you put into the research of the plan, you have started your methods of recording keeping. As I instructed in chapter two, continue to monitor your occupancy, ADR, revPAR, yield statistic and the mix of market segments you attract. Use this information to monitor the effectiveness of your effort. It will be important information to have on hand next year for the creation of another Sales and Marketing Plan.

You will want to have dates set aside for periodic evaluation of the plan. Waiting till the end of the year can be costly. Be objective in your evaluations and take the appropriate corrective actions. Your monitoring can lead to a more streamlined plan in forthcoming years.

The Real Work

Writing the Sales and Marketing Plan was just the tip of the iceberg. **The real work begins now.** You must switch hats, from your research hat to your promotional hat. Don't get too bogged down in the planning stages; come to a decision and act on it. Great people are quick to make decisions and slow to change them. The plan will not increase your occupancy, rate or revenue, it will only show you how you can go about it. You are ultimately responsible, everything about your property reflects on its management.

The Afterword

There aren't any get-rich-quick schemes. All that we accomplish we accomplish through hard work. The hospitality industry is very competitive and new properties are springing up every day making the signs of age on existing properties glaring. The only defense is to combine maintenance, upkeep, service and training with sales, marketing and promotion. You have to take the responsibility to fill your guest rooms.

I am delighted that you have let me help you create an effective plan. I would love to see a finished copy (I'll be certain to keep it top secret) if you care to send one. Let me know what areas of this book you would like to see expanded, ideas that especially worked for your property, any comments or concerns and I will be sure to consult them as I revise this for future printings. Good luck and I wish you much energy as you become the propelling force to a more profitable property. Feel free to contact me, I can be reached at 415-292-5639 or e-mail at corridor@slip.net. I enjoy hearing of your successes!

> Anyone can steer the ship when the sea is calm. — Publilius Syrus

Best Regards,

Joe Wolosz

Index

#

◯, defined, 25

A

AAA, 90
Accor, 13
account grading, 121
action plan, 136, 145, 149, 159
activities, 100
ad hoc group, 48, 118
ADR, 28, 32, 36, 136, 141, 162
ADR, calculated, 29
advertising, 63
airline industry, 32
AltaVista, 89
amenities, 74, 105, 125
America Online, 85
anticipating, 116
association, 49
average daily rate, 28

B

baby boomer, 14
backyard, 56
benefit, 113
Best Western, 15
billboards, 67
billing statements, 66
bottom-up method, 154
brand awareness, 14
brochures, 65
budget, 159
budgeting, 151
business cards, 65

C

card file, 120
central reservations networks, 14
central video recorder, 71
Chamber of Commerce, 51, 99, 109, 148
circulars and newsletters, 66
cold call, 106
collateral inserts, 67
comment cards, 109, 130
commission checks, 65
commissions, 132
commitment, 116
communicate, 112
communication skills, 102
community leaders, 101
competition, 104, 135
competitive analysis, 41
competitive knowledge, 40
competitive set, 40
competitor, 114
competitve parity, 152
complaint, 131
CompuServe, 85
computer software program, 120
computers and technology, 14
concierge, 133
consolidation, 13
Convention and Visitors' Bureau, 52, 105, 109, 148
co-op marketing, 75
Corel WEB.DESIGNER, 88
corporate, 49
corporate volume account, 118
cost containment, 21
credibility, 131
credit cards, 128
customer orientated marketing, 59

D

daily planner, 149
database, 78, 80, 104
date of completion, 140
Days Inn, 13
decor, 127
demand for rooms, 42
differentiation marketing, 58
direct bill account, 58
direct mail, 77
domain name, 87

E

echo effect, 77
ecotourism, 14, 15
education, 99, 127
educational, 46
e-mail, 85, 86
emotional purchase decision, 95
empathy, 113
Encyclopedia of Associations, 81
entrepreneur, 17
envelope, 82
envelopes and invoices, 66
evaluation, 162
event centers, 54
expectations, 126
eye contact, 127

F

fact sheet, 69
failure rate, 136
fair share, 42
feature dumping, 113
feedback, 130
feeder cities, 68, 71
filing system, 120
FIT, 47
fly/drive packages, 47
forecast, 34, 158

forecasting, 141
four P's, 43
franchise, 98
franchising, 59
fraternal, 46
frequent business traveler, 125

G

gift certificates, 101
goals, 98, 137
government, 48
grading, 121
green room, 15
group business, 44
groups, 132
guests, 123
guide book, 90

H

heavy hitters, 80, 105
high demand periods, 33, 158
Hilton, 13
hiring, 103
history, 34, 141
Holiday Franchise Systems, 13
Holiday Inn, 13
hot link, 89
HotMetaL PRO, 88
housekeeping, 102

I

in person sales call, 116
individual business, 45
in-flight magazines, 71
Infoseek, 89
in-house list, 78
inseparability, 22, 43
intangibility, 22, 43
Internet, 86, 87
Internet access, 86

Internet advertising, 85
Internet browser, 86
Internet Service Provider, 86
InterNIC, 87
ISP. *See* Internet Service Provider

J

joint package promotion, 75
junk mail, 77

K

key clients, 105

L

Las Vegas, 13
leads, 103, 117
legalized gambling, 13
level of service, 123
logo, 64
Lycos, 89

M

Macintosh, 86
magazines, 100
mailing list, 78
mailing lists, 79
market approach, 60
market mix, 158
market penetration, 43
market share, 42
marketing mix, 43
marketing, defined, 23
Marriott, 14
McDonald's, 124
Microsoft Internet Explorer, 86
Microsoft's FrontPage, 88
military, 46
mission statement, 138
monitoring, 161
Motel 6, 13

N

names, 130
need periods, 33, 158
negotiating rates, 117
Netscape Navigator, 86
network, 111
networking, 144
news releases, 67
newsletters, 66
newspapers, 100
niche marketing, 44

O

objectives, 93, 136, 139, 158
occupancy, 28, 136, 141, 162
occupancy, calculated, 29
on-line service, 85, 86
organizations, 100
organizing accounts, 120

P

packages, 73
past clients, 103
peak periods, 33
per diem rates, 48
perceived value, 118
percentage of sales, 152
perishability, 22, 43
piggy back sales effort, 75
place, 43
PLC of London, 13
presentation, 102
press releases, 67, 151
price, 43, 60, 124
pricing, 60
print advertising, 70
printed material, 64

INDEX

private line, 129
Prodigy, 85
product, 43
product orientated marketing, 60
product, defined, 23
production, 118
projections, 137
promotion, 43, 63, 151
promotional effort, 63
promotional strategy, 92, 159

Q

QSCV, 124
qualitative analysis, 37, 158
Quality, Service, Cleanliness and Value, 124
quantitative, 159
quantitative analysis, 37, 158

R

rack rate, 35, 75, 117
rate, 115, 124, 126
rate codes, 35
Ray Kroc, 124
referrals, 105, 117
registration records, 79
religious, 46
repeat guests, 74, 79
repositioning, 58, 59, 158
reprints, 70
reputation, 97
research, 135, 151
research methodology, 23
reservation confirmation letters, 65
restaurants, 75
revenue, 136, 141
revenue per available room. *See* revPAR
revPAR, 28, 136, 141, 162
revPAR, calculated, 30
roundtables, 100

S

sales, 94
sales calls, 107, 148
sales professional, 149
sales, defined, 22
salesperson, 98
search engine, 88
segmentation marketing, 57
selling, 93
selling time, 108
series group business, 48
shoulder periods, 33, 158
shuttle flights, 68
SMERF, 45
smile, 127
social, 46
software programs, 120
specialty advertising, 72
sponsoring events, 101
sporting events, 101
staff, 102
standards for performance, 127
strategies, 93, 142, 158
synergetic relationship, 137

T

tactics, 93, 143, 153, 158
task budgeting, 153
teacher, 99
teaser copy, 82
telemarketing, 100, 106
telephone demeanor, 128
television, 71
thank you card, 84
third proposed rate rule, 118
toll free number, 129
Tour & Travel, 46
tour operator, 47, 125
Tourist Welcome Centers, 52
trade journals, 109
trade magazines, 99
trade publications, 68

trade show, 73
travel agencies, 104
travel agents, 105, 109, 125, 129, 132
travel programs, 117
Trends in the lodging industry, 14
truckers, 55

U

user, defined, 23

V

valley periods, 33
value, 60, 124
vendors, 76
Visitors' Centers, 52
volume accounts, 45
volume corporate business, 125

W

web site, 85, 88
welcome note, 125
Windows, 86
word of mouth, 97, 124
World Wide Web, 68, 85, 86, 91

Y

Yahoo!, 89
yellow page advertising, 66
yield management, 32
yield statistic, 32, 36

Z

zero base, 153

Order Form

📄 Fax orders: 415-931-5639
📞 Telephone orders: 415-292-5639
💻 Online orders: corridor@slip.net
✉ Postal orders: Infinite Corridor Publishing
Post Office Box 640051
San Francisco, CA 94164-0051 USA

Please send a copy of HOTEL AND MOTEL SALES, MARKETING AND PROMOTION. If I am not satisfied I understand that I may return the book for a full refund.

Company name:

Name:

Address:
City: State: Zip:

Telephone: Fax:
E-mail:

Signature:
All orders must be signed.

Sales tax: Please add 7.25% for books shipped to California addresses or 8.5% for books shipped to San Francisco, California addresses.
Shipping and Handling: $3.50 for the first book and $2.50 for each additional book.

Payment, do not send cash:
☐ Check
☐ VISA, ☐ MasterCard, ☐ Optima, ☐ AMEX, ☐ Discover
Card number:
Name on card:
Expiration date:

Order Form

📄 Fax orders: 415-931-5639

✆ Telephone orders: 415-292-5639

💻 Online orders: corridor@slip.net

📄 Postal orders: Infinite Corridor Publishing
Post Office Box 640051
San Francisco, CA 94164-0051 USA

Please send a copy of HOTEL AND MOTEL SALES, MARKETING AND PROMOTION. If I am not satisfied I understand that I may return the book for a full refund.

Company name: _____

Name: _____

Address:
City: _____ State: _____ Zip: _____

Telephone: _____ Fax: _____
E-mail: _____

Signature:
All orders must be signed.

Sales tax: Please add 7.25% for books shipped to California addresses or 8.5% for books shipped to San Francisco, California addresses.

Shipping and Handling: $3.50 for the first book and $2.50 for each additional book.

Payment, do not send cash:
☐ Check
☐ VISA, ☐ MasterCard, ☐ Optima, ☐ AMEX, ☐ Discover
Card number:
Name on card:
Expiration date:

Order Form

📄 Fax orders: 415-931-5639
✆ Telephone orders: 415-292-5639
💻 Online orders: corridor@slip.net
✉ Postal orders: Infinite Corridor Publishing
Post Office Box 640051
San Francisco, CA 94164-0051 USA

Please send a copy of HOTEL AND MOTEL SALES, MARKETING AND PROMOTION. If I am not satisfied I understand that I may return the book for a full refund.

Company name:

Name:

Address:
City: State: Zip:

Telephone: Fax:
E-mail:

Signature:
All orders must be signed.

Sales tax: Please add 7.25% for books shipped to California addresses or 8.5% for books shipped to San Francisco, California addresses.
Shipping and Handling: $3.50 for the first book and $2.50 for each additional book.

Payment, do not send cash:
☐ Check
☐ VISA, ☐ MasterCard, ☐ Optima, ☐ AMEX, ☐ Discover
Card number:
Name on card:
Expiration date:

Order Form

📄 Fax orders: 415-931-5639
✆ Telephone orders: 415-292-5639
💻 Online orders: corridor@slip.net
✉ Postal orders: Infinite Corridor Publishing
                   Post Office Box 640051
                   San Francisco, CA 94164-0051 USA

Please send a copy of HOTEL AND MOTEL SALES, MARKETING AND PROMOTION. If I am not satisfied I understand that I may return the book for a full refund.

Company name:

Name:

Address:
City: State: Zip:

Telephone: Fax:
E-mail:

Signature:
All orders must be signed.

Sales tax: Please add 7.25% for books shipped to California addresses or 8.5% for books shipped to San Francisco, California addresses.
Shipping and Handling: $3.50 for the first book and $2.50 for each additional book.

Payment, do not send cash:
☐ Check
☐ VISA, ☐ MasterCard, ☐ Optima, ☐ AMEX, ☐ Discover
Card number:
Name on card:
Expiration date:

Order Form

📄 Fax orders: 415-931-5639
📞 Telephone orders: 415-292-5639
💻 Online orders: corridor@slip.net
📧 Postal orders: Infinite Corridor Publishing
Post Office Box 640051
San Francisco, CA 94164-0051 USA

Please send a copy of HOTEL AND MOTEL SALES, MARKETING AND PROMOTION. If I am not satisfied I understand that I may return the book for a full refund.

Company name:

Name:

Address:
City: State: Zip:

Telephone: Fax:
E-mail:

Signature:
All orders must be signed.

Sales tax: Please add 7.25% for books shipped to California addresses or 8.5% for books shipped to San Francisco, California addresses.
Shipping and Handling: $3.50 for the first book and $2.50 for each additional book.

Payment, do not send cash:
☐ Check
☐ VISA, ☐ MasterCard, ☐ Optima, ☐ AMEX, ☐ Discover
Card number:
Name on card:
Expiration date:

Order Form

📄 Fax orders: 415-931-5639

✆ Telephone orders: 415-292-5639

💻 Online orders: corridor@slip.net

✉ Postal orders: Infinite Corridor Publishing
                        Post Office Box 640051
                        San Francisco, CA 94164-0051 USA

Please send a copy of HOTEL AND MOTEL SALES, MARKETING AND PROMOTION. If I am not satisfied I understand that I may return the book for a full refund.

Company name: _____

Name: _____

Address:
City: _____ State: _____ Zip: _____

Telephone: _____ Fax: _____
E-mail: _____

Signature: _____
All orders must be signed.

Sales tax: Please add 7.25% for books shipped to California addresses or 8.5% for books shipped to San Francisco, California addresses.

Shipping and Handling: $3.50 for the first book and $2.50 for each additional book.

Payment, do not send cash:
☐ Check
☐ VISA, ☐ MasterCard, ☐ Optima, ☐ AMEX, ☐ Discover
Card number:
Name on card:
Expiration date: